On Global Aging

Contributions to Economics

http://www.springer.de/cgi-bin/search_book.pl?series=1262

Further volumes of this series can be found at our homepage.

Kirstin Hubrich
Cointegration Analysis in a German Monetary System
2001. ISBN 3-7908-1352-4

Nico Heerink et al. (Eds.)
Economic Policy and Sustainable Land Use
2001. ISBN 3-7908-1351-6

Friedel Bolle/Michael Carlberg (Eds.)
Advances in Behavioral Economics
2001. ISBN 3-7908-1358-3

Volker Grossmann
Inequality, Economic Growth, and Technological Change
2001. ISBN 3-7908-1364-8

Thomas Riechmann
Learning in Economics
2001. ISBN 3-7908-1384-2

Miriam Beblo
Bargaining over Time Allocation
2001. ISBN 3-7908-1391-5

Peter Meusburger/Heike Jöns (Eds.)
Transformations in Hungary
2001. ISBN 3-7908-1412-1

Claus Brand
Money Stock Control and Inflation Targeting in Germany
2001. ISBN 3-7908-1393-1

Erik Lüth
Private Intergenerational Transfers and Population Aging
2001. ISBN 3-7908-1402-4

Nicole Pohl
Mobility in Space and Time
2001. ISBN 3-7908-1380-X

Pablo Coto-Millán (Ed.)
Essays on Microeconomics and Industrial Organisation
2002. ISBN 3-7908-1390-7

Mario A. Maggioni
Clustering Dynamics and the Locations of High-Tech-Firms
2002. ISBN 3-7908-1431-8

Ludwig Schätzl/Javier Revilla Diez (Eds.)
Technological Change and Regional Development in Europe
2002. ISBN 3-7908-1460-1

Alberto Quadrio Curzio/Marco Fortis (Eds.)
Complexity and Industrial Clusters
2002. ISBN 3-7908-1471-7

Friedel Bolle/Marco Lehmann-Waffenschmidt (Eds.)
Surveys in Experimental Economics
2002. ISBN 3-7908-1472-5

Pablo Coto-Millán
General Equilibrium and Welfare
2002. ISBN 7908-1491-1

Wojciech W. Charemza/Krystyna Strzala (Eds.)
East European Transition and EU Enlargement
2002. ISBN 3-7908-1501-2

Natalja von Westernhagen
Systemic Transformation, Trade and Economic Growth
2002. ISBN 3-7908-1521-7

Josef Falkinger
A Theory of Employment in Firms
2002. ISBN 3-7908-1520-9

Engelbert Plassmann
Econometric Modelling of European Money Demand
2003. ISBN 3-7908-1522-5

Reginald Loyen/Erik Buyst/Greta Devos (Eds.)
Struggeling for Leadership: Antwerp-Rotterdam Port Competition between 1870–2000
2003. ISBN 3-7908-1524-1

Pablo Coto-Millán
Utility and Production, 2nd Edition
2003. ISBN 3-7908-1423-7

Emilio Colombo/John Driffill (Eds.)
The Role of Financial Markets in the Transition Process
2003. ISBN 3-7908-0004-X

Guido S. Merzoni
Strategic Delegation in Firms and in the Trade Union
2003. ISBN 3-7908-1432-6

Jan B. Kuné

On Global Aging

Old-Age Income Systems in the EU and Other Major Parts of the World

With 27 Tables

Springer-Verlag Berlin Heidelberg GmbH

Series Editors
Werner A. Müller
Martina Bihn

Author

Dr. Jan B. Kuné
ABP, Public Employees' Pension Fund
of The Netherlands
Oude Lindestraat 70
6411 EJ Heerlen
The Netherlands
jb.kune@abp.nl

University of Amsterdam
Department of Quantitative Economics
Roetersstraat 11
1018 WB Amsterdam
The Netherlands

The book has been completed on behalf of, and with the financial support of the 'Netherlands Foundation for Pension Studies', The Hague, Netherlands.

ISSN 1431-1933
ISBN 978-3-7908-0030-2 ISBN 978-3-642-50170-8 (eBook)
DOI 10.1007/978-3-642-50170-8

Cataloging-in-Publication Data applied for
A catalog record for this book is available from the Library of Congress.
Bibliographic information published by Die Deutsche Bibliothek
Die Deutsche Bibliothek lists this publication in the Deutsche Nationalbibliografie; detailed bibliographic data is available in the Internet at <http://dnb.ddb.de>.

Softcover Design: Erich Kirchner, Heidelberg

SPIN 10911563 88/3130/DK-5 4 3 2 1 0 – Printed on acid-free and non-aging paper

The lucky family is the one in which the older generation dies before it retires. The unlucky has living retired parents.

Vatter, H.J. and J.F. Walker, *'Support for baby-boom retirees - not to worry'* [1998]

It is better to have two live grandparents than to have two cows.

Kandiyoti, D., *'Poverty in transition,...'* [1999]

Foreword

On the blurb of a publication by P.G. Peterson, a former US Secretary of Commerce [1999] we read, 'the major economies of the world are on a collision course toward a huge, as-yet-unseen iceberg: *Global Aging*. As the populations of the world's leading economies age and shrink, we will face unprecedented political, economic, and moral challenges. But we are woefully unprepared. Now it is time to ring the alarm bell ...'
N. Ferguson and L.J. Kotlikoff [2000] predict that the European Monetary Union will disintegrate in the medium term as the single currency becomes incompatible with the fiscal strains in most of the euro zone countries.
The present monograph discusses that there is reason for concern but not for anxiety or even panic that the adverse impact population aging can have on the economy is inevitable.

Population aging will have a number of sizeable economic consequences. For example, fewer workers relative to the number of elderly will reduce consumption possibilities compared with the level that could be attained without aging. The last 10 to 15 years a relatively large number of studies have been carried out to examine the economic impact of aging societies. Results differ in level and sometimes in direction, obviously dependent on the specification of relationships and the parameters used and probably on preconceived ideas of authors.
Given the considerably different implications of those results for policies continued theoretical and empirical research is needed. Nonetheless the basic mechanism at work has become clear; there is not much time to lose for policy-makers to implement reform measures to address the economic impact of aging and to reduce the distributional burden.

In concluding, we draw on a metaphor applicable on the thirties of the 20th century. At that time we could speak on twin demons, viz. the Malthusian demon of unrestricted population growth accompanied by a stagnating production capacity of the economy vis-à-vis the anti-Malthusian demon of demographic stagnation resulting in insufficient demand. Just as one demon is being chained up, the other one escapes. At the beginning of the 21st century the trade-off is of a different type, viz. between population and economic growth approaching the limits on the one side and a demographic transition resulting in insufficient supply on the other hand. Developed countries a long time ago tamed the Malthusian demon, creating the welfare state of the 20th century. But in doing so, they let enter the anti-Malthusian demon of demographic aging, which they must now tame in the 21st century.

Dr. J.H.R. van de Poel, chairman Netherlands Foundation for Pension Studies.

Acknowledgements

The present monograph is divided into seven chapters, dealing with demography worldwide and the EU-15 countries in particular, the impact of an aging population on the economy, answering the question whether the world population can grow older comfortably, paradoxical effects of long-term trends and short-term issues as well as policies in the face of aging. Its aim is to be of interest to practioners and policy makers as well as the wider academic community.

I am grateful to the Board of Governors of the Netherlands Foundation for Pension Studies for making this publication possible. I like to acknowledge furthermore the Board of Directors of ABP, the Public Employees' Pension Fund in the Netherlands, for allowing me to complete this study and for the opportunities to present my research to symposia and congresses inside and outside demography.

My intellectual interest in demography, population aging and pension finance stems in large part from the time I joined the Amsterdam University in the late seventies of the last century. Thanks are due to W.C.A. Kok for encouraging support. My interest in those topics developed further during the last 15 years when I was with the ABP Pension Fund. I am grateful to A.M. Paulis, J.H.R. van de Poel, E.H.M. Ponds and A.A.C.M. Quix for useful comments. Finally, thanks to Marlène, my nearest, for being so patient and understanding while I was completing this monograph.

The views expressed in this book are my own and not necessarily those of any individual (or the organization he represents), group or institution with which I am or have been associated. Responsibility for any errors remains with me.

Jan B. Kuné

Contents

1 Introductory observations

Lower birth rates and increased life expectancy are in the coming decades significantly shifting the age distribution of population in developed countries towards older persons and in the second half of the 21st century in most developing countries as well.
As a result scope and structure of health care and pension systems are in discussion throughout the world. Apart from lowering benefit levels and increasing contribution rates the issue of funding versus pay-as-you-go is often raised to address the future problems of financing public pensions. Much emphasis is laid on a better functioning of capital and labour markets, increasing labour force participation and a continuing enhancement of productivity. Above all, investments in human capital are of major relevance.

1.1 A growing older society

We are living in an aging society, a statement which can be read and heard more frequently than ever before in publications, political debates and in economic and social analyses. It is a widespread idea that the developed countries today and the developing countries tomorrow with their increasing populations will be confronted with huge economic and social problems. The elderly over 60 years of age are considered as the cause of and a menace for the sustainability of the schemes of old age pensions and the present systems of health and other long-term care.

In former days people were old at ages where they are nowadays are considered as younger and younger. People nowadays not only live longer, but also get older at higher ages only. Or, in other words, people at 60, 70 or 80 years of age are much younger today than they were at those ages in the not so distant past. Particularly at the retirement age between 60 and 65 people are younger than ever before[1]. This implies that the portion of 'older people' in the total population is diminishing. Age alone is far from a perfect measure of aging.
Consequently, never in history people over 60 years of age – till the age of about 80 with present medical technology and health care systems – have been in such good health and capable of many physical and mental productive activities.
It is not advisable therefore to speak of aging societies as societies of decadence and many kinds of problems. Those between 60 and 80 years of age will (and must) increasingly be well integrated in society contributing in many ways to its social and economic development. Individuals and society will both benefit from what gerontologists call active aging.

1.2 The pension burden

The economic costs of a pension scheme or the true measure of the *pension burden* for a society as a whole are the resources or benefits forgone, the resources that are no longer available (for consumption of the non-retired and for investment purposes), as they are being used for supporting the elderly. The costs in respect of any retirement income system are always the same, irrespective how they are financed though they may be distributed differently among generations at date. It will be clear that the costs of population aging cannot be avoided.
Those economic costs are financed by some combination of transfers from labour earnings of the active population (pension contributions), general tax payments and investment revenues (earnings on assets owned by individual retirees or by pension funds). Different approaches to pension financing involve different allocations of pension costs between contributions out of labour income and capital returns.
On the other hand by increasing savings and investments now – the economic costs or the benefits forgone are the reduced current consumption expenditures of the present generations – one is anticipating the difficulties that could otherwise (with no-funding) arise in an economy with a lower national product. This burdens present generations and favours future generations.

The essence of support capability is production. Hence, policies to promote economic growth are the best strategy to cope with the rising costs of an aging population. Assuming the standard of living of the retired population does not stay (far) behind with that of the working-age population, the economic costs of supporting the retired will increase proportionally.
We are of the opinion that the burden of an aging society can nonetheless be easier borne when national product is larger and, otherwise, the burden can be felt as more worrisome when national product is smaller[2]. Increased labour and capital supply and higher productivity are necessary to stimulate economic growth. Higher labour force participation in particular is of great relevance for the elderly as they spend much/most of their income on labour intensive services. You can save and invest in productive capacity, you can save and store durable consumer goods, but you cannot save urgently needed services.

---

1 The blessings of aging are cheerfully applauded by the Geneva Association in its 'Four Pillars Research Program', talking of a counter-aging society.

2 Higher levels of future national product evidently will not alter the spending on old-age pensions in relative terms, but paying for pensions out of a larger economic 'pie', still leaving higher incomes (a grown 'slice' out of the future bigger economic pie) for the non-retired population in absolute terms, is much more comfortable.

Pension finance

More emphasis on funding is generally recommended to cope with the adverse consequences of population aging in the 21st century in the Western world[3]. Evidently a major difference between funding and pay-as-you-go is that funding is generally leading to an additional flow of saving during the period of growing up and under circumstances also in an aging economy with economic growth – ,thereby creating a resource base, which enables higher levels of production and consumption for both future workers and retirees.
If certain conditions are fulfilled, the question whether funding matters and could be part of the solution to the problems caused by e.g. adverse demographic developments (and deteriorating ecological conditions) can be answered in the affirmative (J.B. Kuné [2000]). Funding will be preferential to the extent that it causes national product to be higher.

1.3 Societal issues

Retirement is the product of economic development (predominantly in the 20th century), leading to big changes in the terms of employment, particularly increased leisure during a period towards the end of life, called 'retirement'. As a result, in the second half of the 20th century labour force participation of older men and women declined considerably. Most people retire as soon as it is economically feasible. One may wonder whether it is desirable to put most of the leisure at the end of life. It can be argued that it is advantageous for society and individuals to reallocate leisure some way or other over all ages. Older workers then can take longer work responsibilities, thereby releasing the people in the age groups of 25 to 45 years from the stress arising from combined labour force activities and family responsibilities (caring for small children and elderly parents).

Traditionally most of the burden of subsistence and especially long-term care for the elderly were born by the family. While this burden will grow in the coming decades, today's workers have less children than their parents and grandparents had and family and community networks are rapidly losing the importance they once had. Many present working-age adults have no alternative to public pension and long-term care schemes.
As societies grow older elderly voters have an increasingly growing political power, which causes that government policy measures are increasingly becoming more associated with the economic interests of the elderly rather than the youngsters, which can be harmful for the society.

---

3 Apart from the national economic aspects of aging and pension schemes one of the most prominent features of the current debate is the controversy in respect of pension financing, viz. pay-as-you-go versus funding. This is dealt with by J.B. Kuné [2000].

On a global level a demographically shrinking developed world and expanding developing countries may have geopolitical implications which may lead to a less stable world.

1.4 Budgetary issues

In virtually all the literature on the impact of an a changing demographic structure on the performance of the economy a heavy emphasis is laid on fiscal and budgetary aspects to the neglect of the output of gross national product and its growth. A threatening language has developed, burden of aging, demographic time bombs, dramatic public finance, shrinking welfare state, crises of this and that and all other.
Instead, in this monograph we pay adequate attention to productivity growth, the growth of real product and to average per capita consumption expenditures. In as far per capita welfare still grows, we believe, this will smooth the demographic transition and alleviate the alleged aging problems. We present evidence that could be conclusive to dispose of the idea that a pessimistic scenario is inevitable for most aging countries. Important policy issues, nonetheless, remain. We will dwell on those subject matters in subsequent chapters.

The need to address the budgetary consequences of the aging of the population in the EU-15 countries was formally recognized at the Lisbon European Summit of March 2000. At the next Stockholm European Summit of March 2001 a strategy to address the budgetary implications of aging was outlined in more detail.

In chapter 2 of the present monograph the demography over the first half of the 21st century in the EU-15, the US, Japan, Canada and several less developed countries is shown. In chapter 3 the debate on the impact of an aging population on the economy is summarized. Chapter 4, which is the central part and at the heart of this monograph, presents economic scenarios for the coming decades. It is argued that under realistic and plausible assumptions the EU-15 and other more developed countries can indeed grow old rather comfortably. Less developed countries can gain from the demographic dividend.
Though population aging is far from a problem on a macro-level, nonetheless severe budgetary and fiscal difficulties can arise on the meso and micro-level and thereby a new paradox emanates (chapter 5). An outline of policy measures in the face of aging is given in chapter 6. Chapter 7 draws some concluding remarks.
On behalf of the participants to the Netherlands Foundation for Pension Studies in Appendix E pays close attention to the topic of 'aging in the Netherlands'.

2 Demography

Over the next 50 years the world's population is projected to increase from 6.1 billion to nine billion, corresponding with an annual growth rate shifting from 1.3 percent in 2000 to 0.3 percent in 2050. This contrasts with the 2.04 percent population growth during the 1960's and the 1.33 percent during the 1990's. Projections of IIASA show that the world population will peak at 9 billion around 2070 and then slowly decreases to a median value of 8.4 billion people in 2100, with the 80 percent prediction interval bounded by 5.6 and 12.1 billion[4].

For the coming half century significant growth is projected in Southern Asia and most African countries, moderate growth in Northern America and to a lesser extent moderate in China. The populations of Japan and the European area will decline primarily due to fertility rates far below replacement level. The share of the more developed countries in total world population will shrink.

2.1 Introductory observations

Over the next 50 years, as is well known, the world's population is aging. At the same time that the population over 65 years of age is doubling or more as a percentage of total population in many countries, the working age population of the group aged 20-59 years is declining considerably. The population groups aged 20-59 and 60-64 are shown apart in Table 1, as people in the developed countries generally are retiring far before the age of 65[5]. The young age group of 0-19 years is shown also apart.

Each age group has its own distinct economic behaviour. The young require investment in food, cloths, housing, health care and education. The adults supply labour and spend only part of their income on consumption. The rest they spend to provide for the younger generation and on saving, to a large extent for their own retirement purposes. The elderly, working less or most often not at all, thus becoming dependent again, receive retirement income and health care. When the

---

4 Or, otherwise, there is a 60 percent probability that the world population will not exceed 10 billion by 2100, and about a 15 percent probability that the world population in 2100 will be lower than it is in 2000 (IIASA, *Options*, spring 2002)

5 Labour force participation rates of men aged 60 to 64 have declined substantially since 1960, especially in countries with high unemployment. In virtually all western countries in the early 1960's (male) participation rates were above 70 percent and even above 80 percent in some of them. At the turn of the century the rate had fallen to below 20 percent in Belgium, Italy, France and the Netherlands. It had fallen to about 35 percent in Germany and 40 percent in Spain. In the US the decline from 80 percent to 55 percent was modest in comparison to the decline in the aforementioned European countries. Japan stands out with the smallest decline from about 85 percent to 75 percent.
In Southern European countries the female participation at the turn of the century was around or below 50 per cent, low compared with the ratio in other developed economies. See also subparagraphs 2.2.2 and 2.2.3.

relative size of each of these age groups changes, so changes the relative intensity of their economic behaviour.

People are also living longer. Life expectancy at birth in OECD-countries currently averages about 77 to 78 years, some ten years longer than compared with the early 1960's. In Japan and Singapore life expectancy has reached 80 years, the highest in the world. Throughout the developing countries, wide variation exists in life expectancy at birth, ranging from 75 years and more to less than 45 years.
Trends towards better nutrition, public health, education, working conditions, personal care and advances in health care have contributed to a higher life expectancy and will continue doing so during the 21st century, though unforeseen changes and epidemics may reverse the historical pattern.

Particularly there appears to be a very rapid increase of the number of the very old (those of age 80 and more), with important implications above all for the health care system. The oldest old constitute 17 percent of the population of 65 and over in 2000: 22 percent in developed countries and 13 percent in developing countries. An OECD study [S. Jacobzone et al., 2000] for a number of member countries concluded that publicly financed long-term care costs – predominantly devoted to the oldest old – relative to GDP are likely to rise over the next two decades with on average 3.0 percentage points of GDP (equivalent to about a 50 per cent increase), based on the assumption of unchanged institutionalisation and disability rates. Hopefully, they suggest, trends towards better health among the older population will, at least in part, compensate for the expected increase of overall expenditures on health and long-term care as a proportion of GDP.

2.1.1 Uncertainty of projections

Needless to say that there is always uncertainty in respect of demographic projections, since changes in fertility rates, life expectancy and migration flows are difficult to predict over the long run. Clearly demographic projections are as good as the underlying assumptions on those changes are.
Nonetheless we can be fairly confident about trends in demographic structure over a horizon up to 50 years. Even unexpected shifts in longevity and fertility have not a big impact upon the age profile of the population. There appears to be a slight underestimate over time in projections of the share of the elderly population and an overestimate of fertility rates. As a consequence in nearly all (more developed) countries old-age dependency ratios are higher the more recent the projection[6]. For

6 The US Census forecasts differ from forecasts of UN (1998 and 2000 revision) and from Eurostat forecasts. According to Eurostat the total population of the EU-15 is expected to rise from 376.2 million in 2000 to 386.0 million in 2020, falling to 364.5 in 2050 (US Census 377.8, 384.5 and 350.3 million respectively). On a country level differences in forecasts can be greater. E.g. Germany's population according to Eurostat will rise from 82.1 million in 2000 to 83.3 million in 2020, falling to 76.0 million in 2050 (US Census 82.8, 85.5 and 79.7 million respectively). Italy's population will fall from 57.6 million in 2000 to

Japan, for instance, United Nations projections (revision 2000) of the dependency ratio are 15 percent higher than those projections made in 1998, mainly due to a further increase in life expectancy.

On the other hand the impact of demographic changes on the economy in general and on financial markets in particular is much less certain. Shifts in the demographic structure have many different potential impacts on the performance of the economy, some of which are self-reinforcing and others offsetting.
An elaborate survey of basic demographic data and socio-economic characteristics of countries all over the world at the turn of the century is produced by K. Kinsella and V.A. Kelkoff from the S. Census Bureau [2001].

2.2 Population projections

The U.S. Department of the Census issues many demographic data for all countries of the world. The popular 'middle-series-estimates' are, rather arbitrarily, used in the projection of the retirement issue in the present monograph. Table 1A exhibits population projections and age distribution by 2020 and 2050 in the more developed countries, viz. the EU-15, the US, Canada and Japan. Similar information for Russia and other Eastern European countries is given in Table 1B and for selected Asian, African and Latin American countries in Table 1C.

2.2.1 Population in the developed countries

Over the coming 20 years the population in the EU-15 is still growing slightly. After the year 2020 the EU-population will gradually start to diminish, though at a slow pace. In the EU-15 population decline is about 7½ percent by 2050 compared with 2000: from 377.8 million in 2000 to 350.3 million by 2050.
The number of young persons (aged between 0 and 19) will fall from 86.1 million in 2000 to 61.6 million in 2050, a decline of 28 percent over the first half century. This is the age group that will give birth to children in the following period. Also the population in the working age group declines. Only the population in elderly age groups increase and the increase is highest among the oldest old.
Considerable differences exist among EU-15 member states. The fastest aging societies are those with the greatest declines in fertility and the highest longevity rates.

Three larger European nations, Germany, Italy and Spain have markedly low fertility rates. As a result these countries will lose population over the next half century. Italy will lose the most people in Europe over the next 50 years from 57.6 million to 45 million, followed by Spain and Germany. On the other hand, both France and the UK, Sweden and Belgium have higher than the European average

---

56.0 million in 2020 and fall further to 48.1 million in 2050 (US Census 57.6, 55.5 and 45.0 million respectively).

in fertility rates and, due to immigration, will see constant or only modest population decline over the next 50 years. The Netherlands and Ireland (the latter country not shown in Table 1A) will grow. The demography of the smaller EU countries is shown in Table G1 (Appendix G).

The projection for North America tells us a different story. It shows slow but steady population growth for this region. The population of the United States in 2000 was 275.6 million and will increase to 325.2 million in 2020 and 403.9 million in 2050. The continued growth of the US and Canada population is largely caused by continuing migration and higher fertility rates.
Japan's population due to a rapid and steep decline in birth rates is expected to decline from 126.5 million in 2000 to 101.2 million by 2050. Apart from China Japan's population is aging more rapidly than any population in history.
Population in Russia and Eastern European countries is likely to decrease. By 2020 the population of Russia falls from 146 million in 2000n to 139 million. By 2050 the population may fall to 118.2 million. More pronounced decreases are found in the smaller Eastern European countries. The causes of the projected population decline in this region are below-replacement fertility, relatively high mortality (especially for males) and net out-migration.

2.2.2 Population in the developing countries

With the population of most developed countries decreasing by 2050, tremendous population growth is happening in the developing countries: in India (60 percent in the next 50 years) and in other Southern Asian countries like Pakistan with 89 percent and Iran with 53 percent population growth by 2050. In Latin America Mexico shows the largest population growth over the first half of the 21st century (53 percent), followed by Argentina (35 percent) and Brazil with a minor 20 percent population growth. In Africa population growth rates over the next 50 years differ considerably between e.g. Nigeria (146 percent), Egypt (65 percent), Kenya (28 percent) and South Africa (-25 percent).
One feature that distinguishes most developing countries from the developed world is that demographic aging, which took six to eight decades to manifest itself in the developed countries, will affect the less developed countries in only two or three decades. Developing countries are aging at a much faster rate than the developed world. In addition, population growth in developing countries unfortunately occurs often most rapidly in those geographic areas that are most vulnerable to growth due to an adverse climatic environment, lack of resources and shortcoming social cohesion, giving rise to gloomy economic prospects.

2.2.3 Towards an older population

As a consequence of these demographic developments the number of people aged 65 years and over shows a significant increase relative to the total population.

Table 1A. Total population and age distribution in more developed countries, EU-15, US, Canada and Japan in the years 2000, 2020 and 2050: age groups 0-19 year, 20-59 year, 60-64 year and 65 years of age and over

	Total population	0-19 y	20-59 y	60-64 y	65^{+} y
	(millions)	(	← percentages →		)
	(1)	(2)	(3)	(4)	(5)
EU-15					
2000	377.8	22.8	55.5	5.4	16.3
2020	384.5	19.5	52.8	6.6	21.1
2050	350.3	18.4	45.5	6.4	29.7
Belgium					
2000	10.2	23.5	54.5	5.2	16.8
2020	10.3	20.5	51.5	7.0	21.0
2050	9.3	19.0	46.3	6.3	28.4
France					
2000	59.3	25.4	54.1	4.5	16.0
2020	61.8	22.0	51.1	6.3	20.6
2050	59.0	19.8	46.8	6.2	27.3
Germany					
2000	82.8	21.4	55.6	6.8	16.3
2020	85.5	18.5	53.1	7.0	21.4
2050	79.7	18.6	46.1	6.8	28.5
Italy					
2000	57.6	19.4	56.6	5.9	18.1
2020	55.5	16.0	53.6	6.8	23.6
2050	45.0	15.6	41.9	6.4	36.1
Netherlands					
2000	15.9	24.2	57.5	4.7	13.6
2020	17.1	20.9	52.7	6.7	19.7
2050	16.7	19.7	47.8	6.1	26.4
Spain					
2000	40.0	21.2	57.1	4.8	16.9
2020	39.2	17.3	54.7	6.8	21.2
2050	32.6	15.9	41.1	6.1	36.9

Table 1A. (continued)

	Total population	0-19 y	20-59 y	60-64 y	65^{+} y
	(millions)	(	← percentages →		)
	(1)	(2)	(3)	(4)	(5)
Sweden					
2000	8.9	24.1	53.7	4.9	17.3
2020	8.9	19.8	51.3	6.2	22.7
2050	8.4	18.9	47.0	6.8	27.3
UK					
2000	59.5	25.2	54.2	4.9	15.7
2020	61.4	21.4	52.7	6.3	19.6
2050	58.2	19.4	47.2	6.6	26.8
Other world					
US					
2000	275.6	28.5	55.0	3.9	12.6
2020	325.2	26.4	50.7	6.4	16.5
2050	403.9	26.4	48.1	5.2	20.3
Canada					
2000	31,3	25,9	57.4	4.0	12.7
2020	37,0	21,5	53.4	6.9	18.2
2050	41,4	20,3	48.5	6.2	25.0
Japan					
2000	126.5	20.7	56.3	6.0	17.0
2020	123.4	18.3	49.1	5.9	26.8
2050	101.2	17.4	42.7	6.0	33.9

Source: the U.S. Department of the Census; data can be downloaded from http://www.census.gov/ ipc/www/idbprint.html. Note that projections until the middle of the 21st century are subject to wide margins of error. Marked differences exist between forecasts of UN, Eurostat and the Census Bureau.

Table 1B. Total population and age distribution in Russia and other Eastern European countries in the years 2000, 2020 and 2050: age groups 0-19 year, 20-59 year, 60-64 year and 65 years of age and over

	Total population	0-19 y	20-59 y	60-64 y	65^{+} y
	(millions)	(	← percentages →		)
	(1)	(2)	(3)	(4)	(5)
Russia					
2000	146.0	26.3	55.1	6.0	12.6
2020	139.0	22.1	54.9	7.2	15.8
2050	118.2	18.7	46.5	8.4	26.4
Ukraine					
2000	49.2	25.5	53.2	7.4	13.9
2020	44.4	22.0	55.2	6.7	16.1
2050	37.7	18.6	47.5	7.9	26.0
Poland					
2000	38.7	27.7	55.6	4.4	12.3
2020	38.5	20.8	54.2	7.1	17.9
2050	33.8	18.2	44.8	7.4	29.6
Romania					
2000	22.4	25.8	55.4	5.5	13.3
2020	21.3	20.6	56.2	6.3	16.9
2050	18.3	18.1	44.6	8.0	29.3
Czech Republic					
2000	10.3	23.2	58.5	4.5	13.8
2020	9.9	17.2	54.9	6.4	21.5
2050	8.0	15.5	42.6	7.5	34.4
Hungary					
2000	10.1	23.4	57.0	5.0	14.6
2020	9.5	18.4	55.1	6.5	20.0
2050	7.8	16.5	45.1	7.3	31.1

Source: the U.S. Department of the Census; data can be downloaded from http://www.census.gov/ ipc/www/idbprint.html. Note that projections until the middle of the 21st century are subject to wide margins of error. Marked differences exist between forecasts of UN, Eurostat and the Census Bureau.

Table 1C. Total population and age distribution in less developed countries in the years 2000, 2020 and 2050: age groups 0-19 year, 20-59 year, 60-64 year and 65 years of age and over

	Total population	0-19 y	20-59 y	60-64 y	65^{+} y
	(millions)	(	← percentages →		)
	(1)	(2)	(3)	(4)	(5)
China					
2000	1261.8	33.3	56.5	3.2	7.0
2020	1434.5	25.3	57.8	5.1	11.8
2050	1470.5	21.1	48.5	7.2	23.2
India					
2000	1014.0	43.7	49.3	2.4	4.6
2020	1311.7	34.4	55.2	3.6	6.8
2050	1619.6	26.7	53.0	5.7	14.6
Pakistan					
2000	141.6	51.7	42.1	2.1	4.1
2020	289.0	38.9	53.5	2.7	4.9
2050	267.8	27.6	55.1	5.5	11.8
Indonesia					
2000	224.8	40.5	53.7	1.3	4.5
2020	289.0	32.2	58.1	2.1	7.6
2050	337.8	23.7	55.5	2.8	18.0
Iran					
2000	65.5	47.5	46.0	1.9	4.6
2020	84.2	31.7	59.0	3.3	6.0
2050	100.2	22.5	50.7	7.7	19.1
Turkey					
2000	65.7	39.3	51.9	2.8	6.0
2020	79.7	27.6	58.8	4.4	9.2
2050	86.5	20.8	50.0	6.8	22.4
Brazil					
2000	172.9	39.3	52.8	2.6	5.3
2020	196.9	28.6	57.4	4.4	9.6
2050	206.8	21.7	50.8	6.4	21.1

Table 1C. (continued)

	Total population	0-19 y	20-59 y	60-64 y	65^+ y
	(millions)	(	← percentages →		)
	(1)	(2)	(3)	(4)	(5)
Mexico					
2000	100.4	44.5	48.9	2.3	4.3
2020	128.0	33.6	55.5	3.5	7.4
2050	153.2	25.6	50.6	5.8	18.0
Argentina					
2000	37.0	35.4	50.5	3.7	10.4
2020	44.6	29.9	52.8	4.5	12.8
2050	50.1	22.9	50.9	5.9	20.3
Egypt					
2000	68.4	45.5	48.4	2.3	3.8
2020	90.4	34.8	55.8	3.4	6.0
2050	113.0	26.5	53.3	5.9	14.3
Nigeria					
2000	123.3	54.8	40.6	1.8	2.8
2020	187.4	51.0	43.9	1.7	3.4
2050	303.6	38.6	53.4	2.7	5.3
Kenya					
2000	30.3	55.5	40.3	1.5	2.7
2020	34.0	39.6	54.3	1.9	4.2
2050	38.5	29.2	56.2	4.7	9.9
South Africa					
2000	43.4	43.0	49.8	2.4	4.8
2020	36.7	35.8	52.3	3.5	8.4
2050	32.5	27.7	56.2	4.1	12.0

Source: U.S. Department of the Census; data can be downloaded from http://www.census.gov/ ipc/www/idbprint.html. Note that projections until the middle of the 21st century are subject to wide margins of error. Marked differences exist between forecasts of UN, Eurostat and the Census Bureau.

Developed countries

The proportion of people over 65 years of age (aging ratio) in the EU-15 will increase from 16.3 percent today to 29.7 percent in 2050: from 61.6 million in 2000 to 104
million by 2050. Particularly the proportion of elderly over 80 years of age (the oldest old) increases, whose numbers will rise from 14 million in 2000 to 38 million in 2050.
Considerably higher increases are expected among some of the major continental European countries. In Italy the aging ratio will increase from 18.1 percent to 36.1 percent and in Spain from 16.9 percent to 36.9 percent. In Germany, France it will rise from around 16 percent to 27 à 29 percent and in the UK the increase is less from 15.7 percent to 26.8 percent.
The proportion of children (0-19 years) in the EU-15 is projected to decline further from 22.8 percent in 2000 to 18.4 percent by 2050.
The timing of the demographic change also differs among EU-15 member states. Steep increases occur after 2005 in Germany, Greece, Italy and the Netherlands and some years later in Belgium, Spain, France, Finland and Sweden.
In the US the population over 65 years of age will increase less profoundly from 12.6 percent to 20.3 percent in the first half of the 21st century. Canada takes on an intermediate position between the EU-15 and the US. In Japan the portion of population over 65 will increase considerably from 17.0 percent to 33.9 percent over the coming five decades[7].

Developing counties

In China 33.3 percent of the population in 2000 was of age 19 or below. By 2020 the percentage could fall to 25.3 and further to 21.1 in 2050. This decrease in the youngest age bracket is accompanied by an increase in the percentage of the population aged 65 and above. In 2000 7.0 percent of the population was 65 or older (10.2 percent of age 60 or older). By 2050 the proportion could be 23.2 percent. In Southern Asian countries the proportion of 65 and above will treble or more from about 4½ percent in 2000 to 15 à 19 percent in 2050; the major exception being Pakistan with an aging ratio of 11.8 percent. Turkey takes an intermediate position among Asian countries with a portion of those aged 65 and above of 22.4 percent by 2050.
In most Latin American countries aging is somewhat more pronounced, leading to a fourfold of the aging ratio from about 4½ in 2000 to 20 or more by 2050. The major exception being Mexico, where 18 percent of the population could be over 65 years of age in 2050.
In most African countries the portion of people of age 65 and above will increase considerably in relative terms, but generally not exceeding the 10 percent level in 2050. In Northern African countries and in the Republic of South Africa aging is more pronounced.

---

7 If fertility rates in Japan and Europe remain at the current low level, more than 40 percent of the population of Japan and certain European countries will be older than 64 by 2050.

In 2000 median ages in developed countries are all above the 32-year level, while a majority of developing nations have median ages under 25. The median age in Europe is projected to increase from 37 years in 2000 to about 47 years by 2050. Italy is projected to have the highest median age at that time, with half of its population aged 55 or over.

2.2.4 Old-age dependency

An alternative measure is the old-age dependency ratio – i.e. the number of people aged 65 years and over relative to the number between 20 and 64 years – which in all EU-countries is projected to show a marked increase over the coming decades8. In 2000 the ratio ranged between 19.5 percent (Ireland) and 29.5 percent (Sweden). For the EU-15 as a whole the ratio is expected more to double in the next 50 years from 26.8 percent in 2000 to reach 57.3 percent in 2050. Considerably higher increases are expected among some of the major European countries. In Italy, for example, the ratio, which is already rising markedly, is expected to rising further to reach a peak of 74.7 per cent by 2050; in Spain the ratio is even rising more to 78.1 percent. In Germany and France, it is likely to remain fairly constant in the coming decade, thereafter to rise rapidly before stabilising around 53 per cent by the middle of this century. The ratio is relatively low in the Netherlands and Sweden with 49.0 percent and 50.7 percent respectively.

Conversely, the proportion of children in the EU-15 is falling from 22.8 percent in 2000 to 18.4 percent in 2050. Again, the steepest decline is found in Italy and Spain.

The rise in the US dependency ratio is rather moderate: from 21.4 percent in 2000 to 38.1 percent by 2050, comparable with Australia-New Zealand (not shown in Table 1A). For Japan the ratio is expected to almost triple to come to 69.5 per cent in 2050.

Dependency ratio

The dependency ratio for virtually all developing countries is lower for the entire reference period, but the eventual aging process in many developing countries is projected to be faster than in most OECD-countries. In China the rise of the old-age dependency ratio is also substantial: from 11.7 percent in 2000 to 41.7 percent by the middle of the century. In other Asian countries the increase is markedly less from close to 10 percent at the start of the 21st century to around 25 percent in 2050. In Latin American countries aging is somewhat more pronounced than in Asia (apart from China). The dependency ratio here rises from 10 percent in 2000 to around 30 percent in 2050. Levels ranging between 25 percent and 30 percent are common in the EU-countries at the beginning of the 21st century.

---

8 A still better indication of the economic impact of population aging can be obtained by considering the ratio of persons 65 years and over to employed people as it is they who generate income and pay taxes and contributions.

The dependency ratio rises sharply in Russia and the other Eastern European countries in the period from 2030 to 2050. In the latter year the dependency ratio varies between 48 percent (Russia) to more than 68 percent (Czech Republic).
In African countries we notice hardly any aging with a slowly rising ratio from 8 percent in 2000 to 13 percent fifty years from now.

2.2.5 Towards a shrinking (and older) working age population

At the turn of the 20th century Southern Europe had rather low labour force participation ratios – defined as the portion of the currently employed population to the present population of a particular age group – for the young, whereas Nordic countries had relatively high participation among the elderly. For central age groups, the main differences arise from the behaviour of women, whose labour force participation ratios are lowest in Southern European countries, Belgium and Ireland.
The labour markets will start to tighten when the first wave of the baby-boom cohorts retire in significant numbers in many countries in 2006, when the first baby-boomers reach 60 years of age. Within five years the first labour shortages will arise in countries where early retirement plans in the private and public sector allow workers to withdraw (long) before the age of 65. In the coming three decades the demographic transition will create rather tight labour markets in Japan, Northern America and in Europe (where there is currently still high unemployment at 8 to 9 percent, opposed to about 4.5 percent and 4 percent in the US and Japan respectively).

Developed countries

In the long term the working age population (those aged between 20 and 64) in the EU-15 is expected to decline by 21 percent in 2050 relative to 2000: from 250 million in 2000 to 187 million in 2050. In Italy and Spain the working age population will decline by a substantial 40 percent and 38 percent respectively by 2050. Germany's working population will fall by a moderate 18.4 percent. Again France and the UK are doing better with projected working age population declines of 10 percent and 11 percent respectively. Not only the size but also the age structure of the working age population will change markedly in the coming decades. In Germany the modal age group in 2000 is 36 years old, ten years later it is 46 years and in 2020 and beyond) it has risen to 54 years. The average age of the labour force increase from 39 years today to 42.5 years in 2020 and to a further 43.5 years by 2035 and beyond[9].
Note that it is the combination of a shrinking and aging labour force, which is most relevant for the performance of the economy.
In contrast, the US working population is expected to rise by 32.7 percent over the next 50 years, rather low compared to trends in the past 20th century. Canada is highest among the smaller developed countries with an expected rise in the working age population of 18 percent. Opposed, in Japan the working age

9 A. Börsch-Supan et al. [2001]

population is expected to decline by a considerable 37 percent in 2050. Russia and Eastern European countries also fare rather badly, with a decline in working age population of 27 percent by 2050 in Russia and declines ranging between 25 percent and 35 percent in the other Eastern European countries.

Developing countries

In strong contrast, changes in the age structure are increasing the labour force in virtually all developing countries, leaving the dependency ratio roughly constant despite a rapid increase in the population 65 and over. In India the working age population will increase by a substantial 82 percent by 2050, China follows with an utmost modest increase of 8.6 percent over the first half of the 21st century (Pakistan 159 percent and Iran 85 percent). In Latin American countries growth rates of the working age population differ from 68 percent (Mexico) to 24 percent (Brazil) in the coming five decades.
Very high increases in the working age population are found in African countries, the major exception being South Africa.

2.3 Demographic transition

Population aging results from the change from high fertility and high mortality rates to low or declining fertility and low mortality rates. This worldwide trend is identified as the 'demographic transition'. The transition is characterized first by a decline in mortality, particularly among young children, while fertility tends to remain high. Ceteris paribus, this first phase generates a younger population age structure. During the second phase of the transition fertility declines and populations begin to age. The demographic transition has taken place at different times and takes different forms in different countries. Fertility will continue to decline in all world regions. As a result total world population is not only aging, but also is unlikely to double again in the 21st century, if ever. At the beginning of the 21st century we can discern different patterns of population aging in different countries.

2.3.1 Different patterns of aging

In Western developed countries aging has become a widely discussed phenomenon. The developing countries are aging as well, often at a much faster rate. Today's older countries will experience relatively little change compared with many developing countries. Europe has since decades the highest proportion of population aged 65 years and over among major world regions and will remain the global leader well into the 21st century. With the exception of Japan the world's 25 oldest countries in 2000 are all in Europe. The populations in most of Europe and in Japan not only will age, but also decrease in size over the next 50 years. North America also has a relatively high percentage of elderly people and this share is projected to increase substantially in the coming half century. Levels in Asian and Latin American countries are expected to more than double or even to triple between 2000 and 2050. The proportion of people 65 years and over in sub-Saharan countries will grow rather modestly.

EU-15: slowly declining or static birth rates and static or slowly further declining mortality rates. This results in a relatively modest aging of already aged populations;

US, Canada, Australia, New Zealand: as above for the EU-15, combined with diminishing rates of immigration, resulting in slow to intermediate rates of aging of previously relatively young populations;

Japan: rapidly declined birth rates and static or slowly further declining mortality rates, resulting in world's most rapidly aging society, with life expectancy also among the highest in the world;

Other East Asia: fast demographic transition, low dependency ratios. South Korea and Taiwan must prepare for an aging population, as its baby boom cohorts are quickly getting older;

Russia and Eastern European countries: low birth rates and static or rising mortality rates, leading to moderately aging of already aged populations. Male life expectancy in Russia and other former Sowjet-republics has declined in the last 15 years by about 7 years.

Developing countries: fall in birth rates and accelerating fall in mortality rates, leading to rapid aging in relative terms, but still with rather low dependency ratios.

- *China* shows rapidly declined birth rates (and constant at that low level in future years) and further declining mortality rates, together resulting in a rapid aging of a previously young population[10];
- *other Asia:* South and Southeast Asia have lagged behind East Asia in the demographic transition. South-central Asia has just passed the early phases of the transition;
- *Middle East* and *North Africa:* are at relatively early stages of their demographic transition, having achieved high life expectancy with constant relatively high fertility rates;
- *Latin American* countries (apart from Bolivia, Paraguay and some smaller Middle American countries) are now in an intermediate stage of demographic transition similar to other East Asia;
- among developing countries *Sub-Saharan Africa* is both the youngest continent and the one where population aging is virtually absent; it has not yet or hardly begun the demographic transition. Life expectancy in about 30 African countries is projected to decrease by seven years in the near future due to HIV/AIDS. The working age

10 More information about China is presented in a largely descriptive paper by S. Liu and L. MacKellar [2001]

population is relatively small, making up 50 to 55 percent of total population, whereas in most world's areas that proportion is 60 to 70 percent.

Population aging is primarily dependent on the fertility rate. Mortality rates are falling in virtually all countries of the world. The stage and speed of the demographic transition, hence, are mainly determined by the rate of decline in the birth rate. Birth rates are declining faster in developing countries than in more developed countries. As a result, developing countries are aging faster than more prosperous countries.
Nonetheless, the total world population remains young during the 21st century. Apart from EU-15 and Japan, the proportion of people over 65 years of age remains below or even far below 20 percent of total population in the majority of countries.
A major difference between the developed world and the developing countries is that the developed countries happen to be very rich at the time they are aging; the developing countries may wish they are rich enough at the end of the current century to sustain an older population.

2.3.2 Aging, a feminist issue

Finally it can be observed that aging primarily is a feminist issue as women are normally in the majority in later life. Since in most cultures women marry men older than themselves and men die earlier, a rise in the number of older women also means a rise in the number of widows. Mortality rates in developed countries for women of age 65 and over are about half of male rates. Female advantage in life expectancy at birth varies between 5.7 years (the US) and 12.7 years (Belarus). The average gender gap in life expectancy in developing countries is smaller than in developed countries, varying between 2 years and 6 years (Bangladesh -0.5 years).
Particularly, in developing Asian and African countries, the situation of older women is deteriorating owing to poverty and isolation. In most developing countries older people are among the poorest population groups. Older widowed women often live in isolation in rural areas as their children have migrated (thereby losing their major support network) and the relations not only between generations but also within the community are eroding at a rapid pace. Traditional norms of respect and support are undermined by the values of urban life. The numbers of such isolated and abandoned old people, sometimes male, but most often female, are rising significantly due to the aforementioned developments. In addition, the aging of the rural population may threaten agricultural production.
Low and further declining levels of formal sector employment make social security in most developing countries unrealistic. In addition, more women than men work within non-formal sectors. State pension schemes reach only a small part of the urban population, but are becoming increasingly necessary and urgent.

2.3.3 Falling fertility rates

The downward trend in the fertility rate in European countries after the 1960-1965 period was due to a change in reproductive behaviour which in turn had a broad range of causes, including a shift away from traditional 'family values', greater sexual permissiveness and the advent of modern contraceptives, the growing number of women in the work force (meaning that those who chose to raise up children are faced with the opportunity costs of children), a well developed system of social security (making children dispensable as a form of extended family-based social insurance). In a sense children are luxury goods. In richer households therefore in the future more children will be born opposed to former times characterized by large households being poor.
In virtually all developed countries and in many developing countries as well – notably China, South Korea, Thailand and a dozen Caribbean nations – total fertility in 2000 is at or below replacement level.

The same determining factors of reproductive behaviour will also operate in the future. It is far from sure, therefore, that fertility rates in European countries will increase again to replacement level as projected by e.g. the UN Population Department.
Note also that a fall already occurred in the number of births due to a change in reproductive behaviour rather than to a change in the number of women of child-bearing age gives rise to a further reduction in the number of births in future years even if reproductive behaviour is restored to its initial level. People who have never born cannot raise children.
Policies to increase the number of births by rising the birth rate can only partially be successful. To keep the aging index (i.e. number of people of over 65 years of age relative to the number of 20-64 years) constant, would require considerable increases of the birth rate, for instance in Germany from around 1.3 now to 3.8.

2.3.4 Longevity

Mortality rates declined rapidly and at relatively constant rates in virtually all developed countries over the 19th and 20th century. The age distribution of the mortality decline on the other hand was not continuous over time. In the first four decades of the 20th century – which period was still largely similar to the 19th century – the major part of life expectancy (at birth) improvements resulted from reduced mortality of the younger age groups, particularly the under-fives. By mid-century medical care became more significant and favoured younger and older age groups. All age groups at that time contributed roughly equally to life expectancy improvements. In the last four decades of the 20th century the major part of longevity gains resulted from mortality reduction of the older age groups.

Throughout the first four decades of the 20th century infectious (viral and bacteriological) diseases were the major cause of death, particularly under infants and small children. Better nutrition, housing and adequate public health measures (drinking water, sewerage systems, personal hygienic behaviour) and only to a much lesser extent medical interventions reduced the mortality rate over this time period, particularly the mortality of the young, infants of under-five and older children. By mid-century mortality due to infectious diseases and other vaccine-preventable illnesses continued to decline. New medication (antibiotics) and improved access to it (widespread health insurance schemes arose) contributed most to mortality reduction for the elderly as well as for the young. Over the last four decades of the 20th century mortality reduction has slowed down. Child and young adult mortality are already so low that further improvement can hardly add to overall longevity. High-tech medical treatment and better health behaviour contributed most to the mortality reduction in this period[11], particularly at older ages. Income security systems are also important. Diseases and death are increasingly medicalized.

In the coming decades continued health gain and a further rise in longevity can result from successful medical interventions for cardiovascular diseases, cancer and the degenerative diseases of old age, and above all, from a better life-style and health behaviour (reduced smoking, eating, drinking, and stress, more physical exercise and meditation).
The risks of being subjected to many types of health problems are to a substantial degree linked to socio-economic factors. Hence, people with higher incomes experience more favourable health conditions and live longer than those in the lowest income brackets.

In developing countries by mid-century the introduction of antibiotics and DDT contributed significantly to control bacteriological diseases and malaria that once killed millions of people. Basic medical treatment since the 1960's of the 20th century primarily led to a further lowering of infant and child mortality and only to a lesser extent to an improved health status of the adult and older population.

2.4 Final observations

The most important determinant of the process to a becoming older society is the (rate of) decline in the fertility rate. Or, in other words, the major cause of the demographic transition is to be found at the beginning of the life course, not at the end. But older people are commonly blamed.
On the surface, the aforementioned (demographic) developments may look very ominous, but necessarily they are not[12]. To conclude from rising dependency

---

11 Empirical analysis by F.R. Lichtenberg [2002] provides support for the hypothesis that medical innovation (in the form of new drug approval) contributed most to U.S. longevity increase during the period 1960-1997. In this period life expectancy at birth increased about 10 percent, from 69.7 to 76.5 years.

12 The prospect of growing older populations got the attention of the World Bank [1994], declaring that pay-as-you-go systems around the globe were unsustainable, '... the world is approaching an old age crisis, ...,. Meanwhile, existing systems of financial security for old

ratios that a changing demography places an unsustainable economic burden on societies, given current pension and health care programmes, does not seem justified. In chapter 4 we demonstrate that relatively moderate increases in economic growth rates may more than fully compensate the adverse effects of population aging.
As a consequence, the pension burden may also look much more threatening than it is. Pension crises depend more on political and cultural factors than on demography and economy. From the point of view of the demographic transition, the next 50 years presents the developed world with marked challenges and it presents the developing world with a number of appealing opportunities.

Nonetheless, serious fiscal and budgetary difficulties with adverse effects on the performance of the economy may arise. Secondly, detrimental effects of aging on the proper functioning of the economy via diminished labour supply may depress welfare. Adequate economic policy measures should prevent such effects.
In chapter 3 we turn to the subject of the impact of an aging population on the economy. In chapter 4 the question is answered whether the world can grow older comfortably? Macro- and micro-level of the economy may conflict giving rise to a paradox. Since economies do not behave like well-oiled equilibrium machines, at least not automatically, adequate packages of policy reform measures have to be carried out firmly (chapters 5 and 6 respectively).

---

people are headed towards collapse. The World Bank report urged more pre-funding and a more diversified retirement system with more pillars.

3 The impact of an aging population on the economy

The demographic change (the aging of the population), the costs of supporting the elderly and the way pension plans are financed have an important impact on the performance of the economy as they influence saving behaviour, labour force participation behaviour, technological progress and productivity as well as the level and composition of public spending and the size of the shadow economy. Most of the international literature is rather pessimistic on the impact of population aging on the economy, focusing on the burden that a growing older population will place on the economy in general and the strain on public budgets in particular.

3.1 Aging and capital formation

The study of the relationship between aging, pension finance, saving behaviour and capital formation has produced a considerable volume of theoretical and empirical publications. The primary issue has been whether pay-as-you-go based pension systems reduce aggregate national savings and/or whether greater reliance on funded pension plans would increase national savings. The second question is whether population aging affects other components of saving. The main findings are presented in BOX 1.

BOX 1

How pensions affect personal and total savings[1]

In most developed countries national basic pension plans (first pillar) are predominantly financed on a pay-as-you-go basis. Theoretical analysis suggests a negative relationship between the creation and availability of a pay-as-you-go based basic pension scheme and the level of personal savings. Empirical studies to establish the relationship between this kind of pension plans and the personal as well as the aggregate saving ratio have not produced unambiguous evidence. Introducing pay-as-you-go plans do not seem to have led to depressed personal savings levels nor to less total national savings in a significant way[2]. Most likely public schemes have to a considerable degree replaced 'within family transfer systems'.
On the other hand, pay-as-you-go based systems – particularly when confidence in future pension payments and long-term care is deteriorated – may give rise to a high level of precautionary saving.

Funded pension schemes

There has been much theoretical and empirical research as to whether supplementary funded pension schemes (second pillar) do affect savings and capital investment[3]. Much of the theoretical work is based on the traditional life-cycle theory, its main weakness being that bequests are ruled out. The life cycle hypothesis postulates saving during working age years for retirement and dissaving in retirement.
The substantial degree of acceptance of the modified life cycle hypothesis nonetheless is evident, as virtually all mainstream models use a specification where consumption responds to changes in current income as well as in permanent income and account is given to precautionary saving, possible bequest motives and liquidity constraints.
Mandatory supplementary pension plans are assumed to have a positive impact on the level of personal savings but probably by less than the amount of pension saving itself. On the other hand, tax incentives of supplementary plans tend to reduce government's tax revenues and, ceteris paribus, a higher budget deficit. Empirical evidence shows that funded schemes increase saving fairly relative to the no-pension state – 20 to 60 percent was crowded out, so the net positive effect is 80 to 40 percent of the volume of personal pension savings[4]. See e.g. IBRD [1994]. Empirical studies for several OECD-countries do not show an unambiguous relationship between the growth in pension assets and the *total* national saving ratio, due to decreased offsetting governments savings (needed to implement funded schemes) or reduced private savings (cf. L.H. Thompson [1998][5], E.M. Engen and W.G. Gale [1997].

Hence, the productive capacity of an economy using a funded pension system at least in the short term according to these studies is not necessarily higher compared to an economy using pay-as-you-go schemes only[6]. But a favourable impact can also not be denied on the basis of the same studies. In the long term, however, government savings can be higher than they otherwise (with no-funding) would have been. Tax receipts are less in the short term due to fiscal pension incentives; these taxes are not forgiven, but they are postponed several decades later when pensions are paid out. At that time a higher (government) savings and investment level can result. Though convincing evidence of a strong case for funding on a macro-level is absent, the momentum for a shift from pay-as-you-go to funding remains in many developing countries and former Sowjet-republics in transition. On a micro-level there certainly is a strong case for funding.
We may wonder furthermore whether a lower saving rate, if any, is the real issue, remembering that the aging societies has an unprecedented large capital stock and corresponding high capital intensity. Shortage of skilled labour supply may be a more serious challenge.

1 An elaborate survey of aging, pensions and saving is from R. Kohl and P. O'Brien [1997]. To people from the Netherlands G.E. Hebbink [1996] can be recommended.

2 R.J.M. Alessie, A. Kapteyn and F. Klijn [1997] using micro (panel) data of the years 1986 through 1990 for the Netherlands find evidence supporting the hypothesis of full displacement of household's savings by basic pensions (AOW) wealth. In sharp contrast R. Euwals [2000] concludes that the impact of the AOW on household savings cannot be identified.

3 Apart from the question whether or not funding has contributed to increased savings and investments – compared to what it otherwise would have been – , another relevant question is whether the actual savings level is sufficient and adequate. This question is not dealt with here. It is interesting to note however that the savings ratio and level of investments in e.g. the UK (with a high extent of pension funding) have been lower in the last decades than those in the other large European countries, mostly with a high extent of pay-as-you-go. In macro terms it must be expected therefore that thc UK will face at least the same aging problems, probably worse, despite a high extent of funding in its pension finance system. On the other hand Luxemburg, by far the wealthiest country in Europe with an old-age income system predominantly based on pay-as-you-go is allegedly well equipped to face its population aging.

4 R.J.M. Alessie, A. Kapteyn and F. Klijn [1997] for the Netherlands find evidence supporting the hypothesis of no displacement of free household's savings by supplementary pensions wealth. R. Euwals [2000] comes to opposite findings; the complementary pension schemes have a significant negative impact on household savings, though no full displacement.

5 J.M. Poterba et al. [1998] find strong support for the view that contributions to personal retirement saving programs in the US represent largely new saving.

6 It is interesting to consider more carefully a society with a fully funded pension system but an aggregate capital stock equal to that in a pay-as-you-go based situation. Assuming equal labour input and hence equal output levels, on a macro level there is no difference in national economic performance under both pension finance systems. Thus, on the average there is no difference on a micro level, irrespective of the values of n, g and r in the Aaron 1 rule. Is there a contradiction involved and if so, how it can be cleared up and reconciled with empirical data?
L.H. Thompson ([1988], p. 216), I think, gives the right answer/explanation. Assume an interest rate of 10 percent and a growth rate of population and wages of zero. Thus $r>>g+n$ and funding is to be preferred according to the Aaron-rule. Clearly the individual can obtain a higher rate of return in the private market by escaping from the (pay-as-you-go based) social security program. Thompson: '... assume that we adopt the advance funding approach under which wage earners are forced to come up with $ 90.90 now instead of $ 100 next year. Where do the wage earners get the $ 90.90? Suppose they borrow it from a bank by taking out a home equity line of credit at 10 percent, which costs them $ 100 to pay off next year. Where does the bank get the money to lend? It issues a certificate of deposit to the pension fund, which just happens to have $ 90.90 to invest. What difference does it make whether the system is current cost financed or advance funded? In this example, the difference is one of appearance, not substance: the income claim needed next year to allow the retiree to consume $ 100 comes through a series of private sector transactions if the system is advance funded and from taxes if it is current cost financed.'

3.1.1 Increasing capital intensity

Slower labour force growth may reduce investment demand as a given per capita consumption path can be maintained with less investment. Otherwise, if the saving rate remains constant as labour force growth slows down a higher capital intensity (or capital-labour ratio) results with a declining capital productivity (lower capital returns) and a rising labour productivity (higher real wages). Therefore, an enhanced capacity is created to finance old-age pensions. The younger generation acquires the ownership of assets – behind which the physical capital stock is found – from the aged.

Considering an aging society we may distinguish three situations with an absolutely or relatively declining labour force, accompanied by,

- a reduction in the stock of capital – with constant capital intensity – thereby (in the short term) disengaging resources, which can be transferred to the aged. In this case net investments are negative or, in other words, dissavings of the elderly exceed savings of the youngsters. An aging society can indeed 'live on its capital' for some time. In the perspective of D.M. Cutler et al. [1990] society receives a near-term consumption dividend;
- as far as the allowable rate of capital stock reduction does not exceed capital depreciation, redundant capital can be disengaged rather easily by diminishing or halting gross investments. On the other hand, when allowable disinvestment exceeds capital depreciation practical problems arise in respect of the (physical) feasibility of consuming part of the existing capital stock. Ultimately capital equipment can be sold abroad, thereby acquiring foreign currency by which consumer goods can be bought;
- a reduction in net investments but they remain positive – the capital stock and the capital intensity are still increasing – thereby augmenting in the medium term the volume of consumption for the whole population. In this case savings of the younger population still exceeds dissavings of the elderly, but to a diminishing extent;
- no reduction in net investment, leading to a further increase in the capital intensity of production. Consequently, today less consumption goods can be produced. On the other hand, the higher capital intensity gives rise to a larger labour productivity and a larger future resource base. High flexibility of the economy, viz. a high elasticity of substitution between capital and labour and a high elasticity of savings to the interest rate, makes that a larger part of the capital stock – becoming redundant as a result of the declining labour force – can be absorbed by an increase in the capital intensity.

3.2 Aging and labour supply

Aging of the population tends to reduce labour supply, as labour force participation among the elderly is lower than among the youngsters. One cause of lower participation is the income effect of more generous public pension plans and

a broader coverage of supplementary private plans. Other factors that are important are an increased willingness to retire on grounds of (bad) health, worsening labour market opportunities for the less skilled elderly and, above all, a higher valuation of leisure time.
A slowdown or a possible decline in the labour force will result in a slowdown in output growth. Increased labour productivity growth can compensate for this. However, there appears to be much uncertainty on the impact of (working) population aging on productivity growth. More evidence is presented in BOX 2.

The rapid shift to earlier retirement in many countries has slowed down at the turn of the 20th century and come to a halt; there is even a certain reversal, like in the Netherlands.
Programs to encourage early retirement through disability benefits, lenient unemployment insurance schemes and several early retirement schemes are gradually cut back. Though the trend to earlier retirement has come to a halt now-

---

BOX 2

How pensions affect labour supply

From a theoretical point of view a pension system affects work effort differently to the extent that people perceive social insurance contributions to an unfunded scheme differently from their own savings to a funded scheme. In the first situation with a set of unrelated taxes and income transfers the effect on work effort depends on which of two influences, viz. the substitution effect and the income effect, is the stronger. There may also be an incentive to seek employment in the informal economy where contribution payments can easily be evaded. When people view a pension program as a program of their own pension savings, where future pension payments are closely linked to past contributions, the impact on labour supply, if any, will be substantially less. Nor is there any incentive to seek employment where contribution payments can be evaded.
The impact of the payment of pension benefits – irrespective of how people view its contribution payments – less ambiguously will be a reduction of the work effort of those of retirement age.

Empirical studies examining the impact of income and employment taxes on the labour supply of the working-age population reveal that the impact on the work effort of these taxes for certain small groups of workers can be about 5 percent in response to a 10 percent reduction in net earnings.

Studies examining the factors determining the retirement decision reveal that i.a. the following determinants are of relevance in the individual labour force decision, 1) age, 2) availability and level of an old-age pension, 3) other sources of income, 4) health status, 5) worsening job opportunities and 6) partner's preferences[1].

Older workers generally receive higher wages not because of enhanced productivity but because of seniority systems. Changing age structures undermine these systems and make them unsustainable, necessarily leading to a lower wage level for the older workers, termed demotion. Furthermore, per (older) worker reduced productivity will affect relative earnings again. This will offset the declining job opportunities many (less skilled) older workers are faced with.

Aging and productivity

A fundamental question is the impact of a changing age composition of the workforce on the overall productivity of the economy. The allegedly adverse effects of an aging workforce on productivity and output cannot be supported unambiguously by empirical evidence. According to some research aging will be detrimental to technical progress, as an aging working population turns out to be less dynamic and innovative, obsolete, lack motivation and reluctant to learn ('old dogs cannot learn new tricks'), less prepared to take risks and being less entrepreneurial. Slower growth in the capital stock will increase its average age, a distinct disadvantage in a time of rapid technological growth. It is argued that particularly young workers use new technology. Hence, an older labour force will be dependent on old technology.
D.M. Cutler et al. [1990] on the other hand present evidence to support the alternative view that labour scarcity (in a growing older society) not only induces higher real wages but also investment in human capital (and less investment in physical capital), leading to increased innovation. This is 'the scarcity is the mother of invention' argument. K. Futagami and T. Nakajima [2001] argue that in some specifications of the endogenous growth theory the effects of aging on economic growth might even be positive.

P. Johnson [2002] has pointed out that government-financed opportunities for early retirement often have skewed the choices for it in the past; and that these distortions should be removed and eligibility for public income support before standard retirement age should be tightened. However, in several countries (e.g. the US, the UK, the Netherlands) private (funded) pensions and other sources of capital income constitute the major share of old-age income for many households and, as a consequence, the government's ability to influence the labour force participation of older people declines. Only fiscal measures (grey-tax) may discourage early retirement.

1 See for the Netherlands e.g. C.J.I.M. Henkens [1998], M. Lindeboom [1998] and A.O.H. Heyma [1999]. In OECD Economics Department Working Papers series

several microeconometric analyses of the retirement decision are published, viz. no. 202 all OECD-countries, no. 203 the US, no. 204 Germany, no. 205 Italy, no. 206 the UK and no. 207 the Netherlands. They can be downloaded free (as PDF-file).

---

adays, the continued population aging by itself will lead to a lower future participation rate of the total working population.

3.3 The impact of aging on the performance of the economy

Since one and half decade general equilibrium approaches to the issue of aging, national and multinational, mark a significant departure from earlier partial studies on effects of aging on saving rates and labour supply. General equilibrium approaches enable to take account of market adjustments, which tend to mitigate the effects of population aging. For unchanged pension levels an aging population, for instance, necessitates higher contribution rates in the general equilibrium model, but generally not as high as contribution rates predicted from simple partial projections (BOX 3.). See for a critical but not very convincing review of the adverse effects of aging on the performance of the economy P. Mullan [2000, chapter 7].

3.3.1 Single-country general equilibrium models

One of the most admirable attempts at a general equilibrium approach is the pioneering model of A.J. Auerbach and L.J. Kotlikoff [1987][13]. In a following study of A.J. Auerbach et al. [1989] an adapted model is used to examine the impact of population aging in four OECD-countries, the United States, Japan, Germany and Sweden. The model looks at each country in isolation rather than as a part. Rational consumers live for 75 years, which creates 75 overlapping generations of identical consumers. The model also has a competitive production sector and a government sector. Individuals supply labour under given assumptions about the age-productivity profile and the effects of technical change. They supply capital through an efficient capital market. The social security budget is balanced at all time. A general equilibrium coordinates the three sectors of the economy, ensuring market clearing in all periods. The simulations showed (over the period 1990-2030) a fall in the national saving ratios by 4 percentage points in the US and about 18 percentage points in Japan. Social security taxes (pay-as-you-based pension contributions) will in the same period increase by 8 percent of GDP in Germany and by about 4½ percent in the US.

As a consequence (see also L.J. Kotlikoff et al. [2001]), there is capital shallowing rather than capital deepening. Real wage per effective unit of labour decreases and

---

13 An example of a non-equilibrium study is one by the IMF from 1986 on the effect of aging on social expenditures in various industrial countries (P. Heller et al.)

the real return to capital rises. Nonetheless output growth continues, provided technical progress continues (an annual one percentage point is assumed nowadays), though the economy and per capita welfare will grow less than otherwise, with a constant capital-output ratio would have been the case.
Analyses of saving data in the US demonstrate that the elderly hardly save less than younger age groups (e.g. H.J. Aaron et al. [1989]). Rather, it turns out that an older population holds a larger capital stock (even when the saving rate decreases), thereby causing capital deepening rather than capital shallowing, increasing the marginal productivity and the real wage level of the working population, which creates favourable conditions for solving the distributional problem of retirees and younger age cohorts.

3.3.2 Multi-country general equilibrium models

The multinational equilibrium approach in turn is a marked departure from the single country model. The first effort at modelling the impact of aging on a global economic level was made in 1990 by the IMF (P.R. Masson and R.W. Tryon). The study used a general equilibrium, multinational model to calculate the effects of population aging and the impact of a declining working population in a number of developed countries on some economic and fiscal variables, particularly on savings. In all countries under study aging has a negative impact on real economic output relative to the baseline, ranging from a modest 1.6 percent in France, 5.8 percent in Germany and a highest 13.2 percent in Japan by 2025.

In 1998 the OECD made a more ambitious effort to calculate the macroeconomic impact of aging populations using a general equilibrium, multi-country global model (D. Turner et al.). The study relied on OECD's 'minilink' model. The model has five distinct regions, the US, Japan, the EU-15, a combination of various fast aging countries of the rest of the world and a combination of slow aging countries. Regions are linked through international trade in goods, services and financial assets.

The authors found a trend of a declining pace of increase in living standards (i.c. per capita GNP). Living standards, the variable that policy makers concerns most, will continue to rise with the aging of the population in the OECD-countries, but they will rise less than otherwise would have been the case without aging, 23 percent lower in Japan, 18 percent lower in Europe and 10 percent lower in the US by 2050 in relative terms. For the US and Japan the employment impact explains almost 100 percent of the total impact of the aging of the population on potential national product. For the EU-15 the employment impact generates two thirds of the total impact and changes in the capital stock the other third.

Other studies

Following the IMF and OECD, the European Commission (K. McMorrow and W. Roeger [1999]) also carried out a general equilibrium, multi-country study. It

models outcomes for the 15 members of the European Union in the aggregate and the US and Japan separately. The study finds an almost identical impact of aging on living standards as the OECD-study does, a cumulative decline of 22 percent in Japan, 19 percent in Europe and 10 percent in the US relative to the situation without aging, in all regions mainly generated through changes in employment[14]. Next, the study simulates the effect of combining various reform measures, viz. keeping budgets close to zero or in surplus, adequate pension reform, raising labour force participation rates by 10 percent in Europe and regulatory changes to boost productivity. If all these policy measures are adopted, then Europe can entirely overcome the impact of aging and even increase its growth above the baseline scenario by a cumulative (slight) 5 percent in 2050.
A follow-up study by the same authors has been published at the beginning of 2002. A 'preferred policy scenario' for the EU-15 is presented; more details are given in Appendix F.

IIASA [L. MacKellar et al., 2002] in an excellent study gives evidence for Japan. The macroeconomic consequences of Japan's population aging are that the growth of per capita GDP decelerates from 1.6 percent in 2000 to 1.1 percent in 2030-2040, turning up to 1.4 percent by 2050 as decline in the labour force slows. D. Turner et al. foresee a markedly lower per capita GDP growth rate of 1.2 percent in the coming decades, declining to 0.8 percent in 2050. The difference can at least in part be explained by a rising output-capital ratio from roughly 2.6 to 3.5 over the coming half century (despite a declining aggregate savings rate over the next 50 years from 7.1 to 1.5 as a percentage of GDP) as opposed to a constant capital-output ratio in the study by D. Turner et al. Hence, in the IIASA model, the higher capital intensity implies a gradual increase in the average productivity of the labour force. The rate of return on capital is rising in the IIASA projection from 5.8 percent in 2000 to 2.6 percent in 2050. D. Turner et al. project a slight increase in the rate of capital return to 5.4 by 2050. Thus, it appears that remarkable differences exist between alternative models both in estimated level and sometimes projected trends.

3.3.3 Concluding observations

An illustration of the often-opposed results of a partial and a general equilibrium analysis can be found in the current social security and pension reform debate. The major concern – sometimes somewhat hysterical – here has been about the burden

14 Similarly D. Miles [1999], '... the European average level of per capita GDP is just under 25 percent lower by 2050 than it would be with an unchanged demographic structure.' T. Chauveau and R. Loufir [1997] find evidence of a declining per capita output varying between 7 percent (the US) and 22 percent (Italy) in 2050 compared to 2000. If a yearly productivity growth of 2 percent is taken into account, per capita output by 2050 is 2½ to more than 3 times as high as in 2000.
For the Netherlands D.P. Broer [2001] concludes that the projected scarcity of labour results in an output loss of 12 percent by 2040 relative to the steady-state path of the economy.

on the (small) baby bust generation that a pay-as-you-go financed defined benefit-system imposes on it. H. Bohn [1999] convincingly demonstrates that for plausible contribution rates and elasticities of factor substitution, small cohorts are actually better off than large cohorts. This is because small cohorts enjoy favourable wage and interest rate movements even though they face relatively

---

BOX 3

Population aging and economic performance

The first detailed analyses of the economic effects of an aging population have been carried out about one decade ago by e.g. A.J. Auerbach et al. [1989], P.R. Masson and R.W. Tryon [1990], P.R. Masson [1991], R.C. Fair and K.M. Dominguez [1991][1]. They examined the macroeconomic effects of population aging in a number of developed countries using general equilibrium models, the middle two employing the IMF's multi-regional econometric model. Demographic variables are determined exogenously and the aim is to explore the effect of aging on i.a. saving and consumption propensities, government expenditures and tax revenues, social security expenditures and health care provision, labour supply and real wage rate, capital supply and real interest rate, exchange rates, the current account of the balance of payments and international capital flows.

Factors of production

The simulation results indicate that aging could have a significant negative effect on the national saving rate, leading to lower capital formation, productivity and employment. A large negative effect of aging on private savings in Europe is calculated by Miles [1999; 2002[a]]: the saving rate in the base case scenario decreases from 14.5 percent in 2000 to 4.5 percent or less in 2050 (mainly dependent on the assumed productivity growth). These results however are as plausible as are the underlying assumptions, and one of the key assumptions in these models is that savings rates decline with age. The theoretical justification for this assumption derives from the life-cycle model with no bequest motive, where assets are accumulated over the working years and used during retirement. The empirical foundations however are weak or contradictory: the elderly save as high a proportion of their income as the younger age groups or even more.

The aging of the labour force population probably will not have much effect on its flexibility in respect of e.g. mobility, ability to adapt to new techniques and innovative capacities, and thereby on the overall

performance of the economy [P. Johnson & K.F. Zimmermann, 1993; P. Johnson, 2002; R. Disney, 1996].
Another assumption of utmost and predominant relevance is the effect of aging on the rate of technological progress. Technical progress could decrease due to a lesser dynamism of an aging population. On the other hand innovation can increase as labour becomes more scarce [D.M. Cutler et al., 1990]. The last author concludes that population aging will not bring about major problems for productivity. The models of the OECD [1998[b]] and the European Commission [1999] also assume no impact of population aging on productivity growth.

Simulations using general equilibrium models are pioneering attempts to examine the economic impact of aging in developed economies, demonstrating the complexity of the relationships between population age structure and economic performance. Assumptions about e.g. saving behaviour, technology, global developments are crucial. Small changes and differences in initial assumptions produce large differences in long-term simulation results.

It is often argued that unfunded public pension schemes are increasing the depressing effects of aging on savings. In the life-cycle framework public pensions can be regarded as a form of implicit wealth accumulation, whereby the need for old-age savings is reduced. M.S. Feldstein [1974, 1995] has produced a lot of evidence. His findings have been disputed. Other studies indicate that the effects, even if negative, may be small[2].

International relations

Differences in aging patterns between countries will result in prolonged swings in the current account of the balance of payments against each other and against other parts of the world, leading to large changes in their net foreign asset positions. Note the situation in which aging might lead to dissaving and a deficit on the current account. Clearly not all more developed countries (going through the same aging process) can show simultaneous declines in the current account position. General equilibrium mechanisms therefore are introduced in the model. Recent examples are Brooks [2000[b]] and the INGENUE world model [2002], where six relatively homogeneous regions are economically and financially perfectly integrated.

The older a society is, the greater the per capita expenditures on social security will be, and the larger the part of pay-as-you-go based pension systems the greater the share of unit labour costs and the higher the prices for goods and services. The higher the prices of internationally traded goods, the less favourable the competitive position in world markets.

Monetary policy

E.P. Davis [2002] has pointed out that the process of population aging will involve major shifts in financing, which may give rise to financial turbulence. They are brought about by risks arising from the overall macroeconomic development, the difficulties of pay-as-you-go financing, the risks arising from the manner of funding via institutional investors and the risks arising from the asset accumulation during funding.
Therefore, D. Miles [2002^b] raises the question whether monetary policy should be different in a greyer world. Nowadays, European monetary policy is directed almost exclusively at controlling inflation. That inflation target is based upon measures of consumer prices and do not reflect asset prices. The elderly population is likely to be relatively more concerned about asset-price level than about consumer prices. Do objectives of monetary policy have to change in the future?

1 During the nineties several other interesting studies appeared, e.g. J.A. Bikker [1996], A. Börsch-Supan [1996], S.K. Chand and A. Jaeger [1996], D. Roseveare et al. [1996], W. Leibfritz et al. [1996], OECD [1996, 1998], T. Chauveau and R. Loufir [1997] and D. Miles [1997, 1999].

2 It appears, as observed by H.J. Aaron [1982, p. 28], that '... a person determined to find a respected theoretical argument to support a preconception can find one, and that a person without preconceptions will find a bewildering diversity of answers in economic theory about whether social security is more likely to raise or to lower consumption or labour supply.
To get by this theoretical impasse, one turns with hope to the empirical research for measures of observed behavioral responses. As will become clear, most of these hopes remain unfulfilled.'

---

high contribution rates to pay for the pensions of the preceding larger cohorts under a pay-as-you-go based DB-system. Conversely, large cohorts are worse off than small ones: their high labour supply drives down the wage rate when the cohort is young and pension asset prices go down when the cohort wants to sell these assets when old. This is clearly beneficial for the young small cohorts.

Conventional partial equilibrium analyses make long run projections of future wage and interest rates by extrapolating past trends and ignores endogenous factor price effects, which can be seriously misleading. General equilibrium analyses, hence, are to be preferred.
It can not be shown unambiguously from theoretical analyses that population aging adversely affects economic performance, though it seems likely – mainly due to a shrinkage of the labour force – that in the first quarter of the 21st century (and more seriously during the second quarter) growth rates of GDP in most OECD-countries will slow down. At that time it is only productivity that drives all growth.

The effects of aging on the performance of the economy, a (if any) gradual shift to a funded system and other reform measures will have important implications for domestic and international capital markets. First the scope and structure, the breadth and depth of worldwide financial markets. Secondly, the impact on prices and rates of return on various types of assets in different geographical areas as well as across time. This subject matter is not pursued here. Reference is made to papers presented at a workshop, organized by CPB (Netherlands Bureau for Economic Policy Analysis), *'Ageing and international capital flows'*, The Hague, autumn 2001 (www.cpb.nl/nl/activ/ageing/).

3.3.4 Productivity growth the most important factor

It will be demonstrated below (chapter 4) in a simple scenario-analysis for (developed) aging societies that a rather moderate increase in labour productivity suffices to offset the negative impact of population aging on average per capita consumption or general standard of living[15]. Assuming a growth rate of labour productivity of 1¾ percent per year ensures significant welfare increases for both working-age groups and pensioners. Productivity growth, hence, appears to be the single most important factor in alleviating the costs of global aging.
This result markedly contrasts with findings from e.g. a general equilibrium approach of A. Börsch-Supan [1996], investigating the impact of population aging on saving, investment and per capita consumption in the OECD-area. Per capita consumption – the 1990-index being 100 – in the latter study decreases in the coming decades to 92 à 87, depending on the rate of technical progress (which function is working via labour force growth and its average age).
On the other hand D. Turner et al. [1998] observe that '... living standards will continue to rise in the main OECD regions, despite ageing. Thus, for example, living standards, expressed in terms of per capita GNP could be about 80, 90 and 100 percent higher by 2050 in the US, Japan and the EU respectively than at the turn of the century. Nonetheless, the implied rates of growth in living standards (in the 21st century) are markedly slower than in previous decades [...]. Furthermore, a suitable package of reform policies should go a long way to re-establishing earlier growth trends.' With appropriate reform measures resulting per capita GNP could be even 202, 227 and 264 by 2050 in the US, Japan and the EU-15 respectively (1995=100).

Provisos

The only proviso that can be made is that society in 2050 is less affluent than it otherwise without aging would have been. Living standards would be 23 percent lower in Japan, 18 percent lower in Europe and 10 percent lower in the US than would otherwise occur without aging. Living standards will also be lower when compared to recent historical trends, which are based on gains in productivity of 1,75 percent annually in the US and 2 percent both in Japan and the European

15 D.M. Cutler et al. [1990] also argue that a moderate rate of technological progress might be sufficient to offset a decline in the living standard due to aging.

Union. When productivity trends converge to 1,4 percent, the shortfall in living standard gains is 35 percent in Japan by 2050, 24 percent in the US and 28 percent in the European Union.

Note, however, that a decline in the rate of economic growth may not matter, at least not seriously, as long as per capita income rises even when the size of the population declines. In contrast, an overall decline in the economy with lower per capita incomes may have a serious negative impact on at least some segments of the economy as well as on the value of some real and financial assets. On the other hand, the higher the rate of growth of the economy, in our view the less acute the distributional problem will be.

3.3.5 Remaining research questions

We can be certain that the study of the impact of demographic development on the economy will continue to be high on the research agenda in the first half of this century. Research topics include,

- the validity of the (modified) life-cycle model: the saving decisions of those people belonging to the labour force and of elderly pensioners and the channels through which they work by e.g. combined cross-section and time series analysis;
- the effects of aging on the productivity and factor prices of labour and capital, and, above all, the effect of labour scarcity on technological change possibly inducing a reallocation from physical capital to human capital;
- the (allegedly adverse) effects of higher tax and contribution rates during the period towards an aging society, and particularly during the transition to a higher degree of funding in pension finance;
- the burden imposed on present and future generations: knowing who pays how much and how long and when, and who benefits. This research object is termed generational accounting;
- are differences in time profiles of demographic changes and in productive capacity in different worldly regions large enough to be mutually advantageous, given the current and foreseeable extent of international economic and financial integration? Can large discrepancies exist – and how long – between domestic saving and domestic investment in aging countries (large net external positions)? The question of the sustainability of such developments arises.

3.4 Final observations

Economists do not agree on how to construct macro demo-economic models and how to specify relationships between demographic, economic, fiscal and social variables and above all, do not agree which assumptions have to be made about e.g. longevity, retirement age, wage level, inflation rate, labour force participation, interest rate, equity premium and productivity growth. Small differences in these assumptions, particularly productivity changes, can produce very different results[16].

Research done by the OECD [1998[b]] and the European Commission [1999, 2001, 2002] shows that with the right combination of economic and social policy measures it is possible to more than compensate for the adverse effects of population aging on the economy. There is room for a further increase of welfare.

Looking at the issue of aging and the performance of the economy the uncertainties are great and compounded. We know very little about the impact of population aging on household behaviour, social security arrangements and the society as a whole. The question to be answered is how people will behave in situations that haven no historic precedent? What will be the life expectancy in 2050? At what age people will retire, later or earlier than they do now? Are people willing and able to invest more in their human capital, thereby contributing to sustained productivity growth? How will governments in any given country respond to the increasing costs of public (pay-as-you-go based) pension, health and other long-term care expenditures, by cutting benefits and provisions, raising taxes and contributions or borrowing on the capital market? And how will governments respond to the challenge to enlarge the resource base, by stimulating the labour force participation, enhancing the knowledge, skills and abilities of the workers or increasing the capital intensity of the economy?

16 More pronounced (H.J. Aaron [1982]), '... a person determined to find a respected theoretical argument to support a preconception can find one. And that a person without preconceptions will find a bewildering diversity of answers in economic theory about whether social security is more likely to raise or to lower ...'

4 Can the world population grow older comfortably ?

The central question in this monograph is whether the world in general and the aging developed world and the EU-15 in particular can afford to get older and to pay for its pensions, health and other long-term care. The answer, we believe, is highly likely to be affirmative. This statement is explained in more detail in the following paragraphs.

4.1 Scenarios of the demographic transition in developed countries

The size of birth cohorts has a significant impact on labour and capital markets. The question arises what this impact is particularly in the more developed countries under consideration in the coming decades? Some tentative lines of thinking about developments of population, labour market and capital market in the coming decades are exposed in Table 2.

The baby boom generation is pronounced in the EU-15, the US, Canada and Japan, in Russia and the Eastern European countries and apart from China almost absent in the developing countries. The baby boom generations result in a bulge in the age structure, a demographic wave that passes its way through the population.
Taking 1955 as the year of birth of the average baby boomer and 1985 as the year of birth of the average member of the baby bust generation in the EU-15, then in the *near* term – the years between 2000 and 2015 – the representative baby boomer will be between 45 and 60 years of age and the average baby buster will be aged from 15 to 30. The next generation is still unborn.
In the *medium* term, 2015-2030, the average baby boomer is of age 60-75 – his parents are no longer living in this period – and the average baby buster is of age 30-45. The next generation is then between 0 and 15 years of age. In the *long* term – the period 2030-2050 – the average baby boomer will be older than 75 and the average baby buster is between 45 and 65. The next generation ages from 15 to 35.

4.1.1 Aging and the labour market

The population groups over 60 years of age are characterized by labour force exit and pension assets divestiture. They sell these assets to members of the next generations who are between 30 and 60 years of age, who are then in the labour force and who are accumulating pension capital for themselves. Pensioners start selling assets after 2010/2015 and increasingly in the following decades.

Table 2. Prospects in respect of population, labour market and capital market in the EU-15; near term, medium term and long term

Near term (2000-2015)

POPULATION:	
'last' generation:	75^+, sellers assets
baby-boom generation:	45-60y, buyers assets
baby-bust generation:	15-30y, leading edge cohorts entry labour market
'next' generation:	unborn
LABOUR MARKET:	gradual tightening; increasing participation rate, higher level of wages, particularly in respect of young labour supply
CAPITAL MARKET:	structural large demand for assets; rather high asset prices; higher saving and investment levels.

Medium term (2015-2030)

POPULATION:	
'last' generation:	dead
baby-boom generation:	60-75y, exit labour market, sellers assets
baby-bust generation:	30-45y, buyers assets
'next' generation:	0-15y
LABOUR MARKET:	tight, bottlenecks; high participation rate, rather high level of wages
CAPITAL MARKET:	relaxing, baby-boom generation seller of assets to the less numerous baby-bust generation; lower real interest rate, lower asset prices; constant or slightly lower saving and investment levels.

Long term (2030-2050)

POPULATION:	
baby-boom generation:	75^+, sellers assets
baby-bust generation:	45-65y, buyers assets
'next' generation:	15-35y, entry labour market
LABOUR MARKET:	normalized; high participation rate
CAPITAL MARKET:	relaxing, baby-boom generation seller of assets to the less numerous baby-bust generation; structural low real interest rate and low asset prices; constant or slightly decreasing savings and investments. After 2050 towards new equilibrium values.

There is a close relationship between cohort size and *labour market* conditions. In the *near* and medium term the labour market is becoming gradually tighter as the leading edge baby boomers are leaving and the far less numerous young baby-bust cohorts are entering the labour market. In the *medium* term the next baby boom generations are leaving the labour market. As a result labour is becoming scarcer whereas capital is relatively abundant. Capital intensity increases due to a sustained high level of investment; labour productivity and wage rates will rise.
Basic economic relationships in a neo-classical economy are dealt with in Appendix D.
Note that the baby boomers are leaving work when middle aged and the next generation probably will do the opposite, enjoying life when young, entering labour force afterwards and leaving working life at higher than middle ages, later than their parents did. This partly offsets swings in the wage level.

We assume that the participation rate of the working age population in the EU-15 will rise with about 5 to 6 percentage points by 2020. Hence, with a slightly decreasing working age population the work force will increase over the two coming decades at a yearly rate of about 0.4 percent. In the *long* term with negative population growth and unchanged participation ratios the work force will decline in relative and absolute terms. Differences exist between EU-15 member states, as pointed out in paragraph 2.2.
Labour scarcity will induce wage increases. Higher wage rates can have two contradictory effects, first (in a world of global competition) inducing capital substitution and hence, further productivity and employment growth. Secondly, higher wages can harm competitiveness, impede productivity growth, leading to diminishing investment and increasing unemployment, particularly of low-qualified labour.
The same argument holds for a relatively low wage rate: either inducing labour substitution and lower productivity growth or contributing to a strong competitive position.

4.1.2 Aging and the capital market

Of major relevance is also the behaviour of *capital markets* in reaction to demographic developments. In the *near* future there will be a continuing demand for assets from the baby boom generation. Asset prices will remain rather high. Savings and investments continue to grow; a less increasing labour supply will give rise to a higher capital intensity and a lower rate of return to capital, but also to inflationary forces, which work in the opposite direction[17].

---

17 The projection of more scarce labour and more abundant (physical) capital implies a lower (long-run) marginal product of capital, which is the source of returns to financial assets. Or, in other words, returns to financial assets must reflect the returns on capital investment over the long run.
The decease in the rate of return on capital in Germany, resulting from both population aging and more funding in pension finance is estimated by A. Börsch-Supan et al. [2001] to be 1 percentage point (assuming a closed economy). International diversification can

In the *medium* term asset prices and the expected return on capital will be permanently lower, when the younger baby boomers are leaving the labour force and the less numerous cohorts of baby busters are entering, further raising the capital-labour ratio.

In the *long* term the tail-end baby boomers and the (leading edge) baby busters continue selling assets to the next baby bust cohorts. Asset prices will fall further, even a crash or market meltdown may occur. Note that this problem arises in much more acute form with personal (individual) pension accounts – where on approaching retirement age investments are switched from equities to bonds – than in collectively organized pension funds with infinite horizon. R. Brooks [2000[a]] finds (simulation) evidence for the US of significant asset market effects, with the expected return on retirement savings of (tail-end) baby boomer cohorts about 10 to 20 percent below returns to earlier generations. Past capital returns evidently are not a good guide, let alone a guarantee, to returns that can be expected over the coming demographic transition.

Note that the large capital accumulation of the baby boomers induces the next generations to reduce their savings anticipating immense inheritances. The next (leading-edge) baby bust generation likely increases savings not until the second half of their working life, when all the former (from leading edge to tail-end) baby boom generations want to sell their pension capital. This reinforces the fall in asset prices but offsets at least in part the decline in interest rates or induces them to rise.

By and beyond 2050 a new equilibrium level arises as the baby boom and the baby bust cohorts pass their way through the age distribution. Decreased savings and investments match with the decline in the rate of investments required to achieve a constant capital–output ratio. Hence, the rates of return to labour and capital stabilize.

4.1.3 Labour force participation

Of the total population in 2000 in the EU-15 about 42 per cent was actually employed. The labour force participation, defined as the ratio of the currently employed population to the present population of age groups 20-64 years, at that time was 0.69, which is lower than e.g. in the US and Japan. There appears to be ample room for a further increase of labour force participation in virtually all European countries, by reducing the unemployment rate, curtailing pervasive early retirement, increasing the female participation and that of allochthones in the labour force[18].

---

improve the return on capital considerably. If capital is freely mobile within the EU-15 the decrease in the return to capital is only 0.2 percentage points.

18 The Netherlands Bureau for Economic Policy Analysis (CPB) thus expects a considerable increase in the labour force ratio in 2020 (in 2000: 0.71). A fraction of 0.77 of the working age population – or 0.45 of the total population at that time –

The baseline scenario of the EU Economic Policy Committee's *'Progress Report on the impact of ageing population on public pension systems'* [2000] therefore assumes that participation rates in the EU-15 gradually converge from 0.69 in 2000 to 0.75 in 2020 and 0.78 in 2050 (the latter figure being the performance in the US and Japan at the beginning of the 21st century and commonly considered as full employment). Considerable differences exist between EU-15 member states at date. Rather high participation rates are found in the UK and Sweden; Germany and the Netherlands take an intermediate position and relative low rates exist in France, Spain, Belgium and Italy. Hence, Italy expectedly will show the steepest increase in labour force participation in the near future, followed by the other countries, giving rise to considerable policy challenges[19].

In the present monograph a somewhat less optimistic scenario is used where countries with initial low participation rates, e.g. Italy, Spain, Belgium, raise working force participation with 7 to 8 percentage points at best to 0.67, 0.71 and 0.70 respectively. For the sake of completeness also a high employment scenario is presented, characterized by a labour force participation ratio of 0.78 in all EU-25 member states by 2050.

4.1.4 Labour force productivity[20]

Growth in labour productivity in European countries in the seventies and eighties – a period with rather low productivity growth, but still higher than in the nineties – amounted to 2 percent per year approximately (Englander, A.S. and A. Gurney [1994]). On the one side, it seems to be reasonable to take the productivity growth in these decades as a lower bound for future productivity growth. On the other hand, in the face of feasible negative consequences of population aging on labour supply, labour productivity and saving/investment decisions as well as the falling of the productivity growth due to an aging working population and a higher part of services in national product, that 2 percent productivity growth rate, particularly after 2020, must more likely be considered as an upper bound ceiling. The baseline scenario in the present monograph, therefore, assumes that a slightly less

---

can then be employed (CPB [1996], CPB/CBS [1997]). Note that – in calculating the results shown in Tables 3, 4 and 5 – the heroic assumption of an unchanged average number of hours worked per worker per year has been made. It can be expected that the number of part-time workers will increase further in relative terms in the coming two decades.

19 Under the Lisbon scenario of the EU Economic Policy Committee's study [2000] there are even more improvements in the labour force participation. Both male and female participation rates rise and converge to 83 by 2045. This assumes substantial increased participation by the elderly. Unemployment declines to 4 percent for both males and females by 2045.

20 The extent to which higher output levels ease budgetary pressures depend on how higher output is achieved. If output is primarily increased through higher utilisation of labour the level of pension outlays relative to GDP can be lower. If, instead, output growth is brought about by productivity growth, the ratio of pension spending to GDP will not change significantly in those countries where pension benefits are linked to wage level.

1¾ percent yearly growth rate in per worker production can be realized in the coming half century[21]. Note that those estimates are guestimates as it practically impossible to accurately project productivity growth.
In paragraph 4.3 below scenario findings are presented.

4.1.5 Alternative scenarios

A less optimistic scenario, however, assumes – maintaining the previous 1¾ percent growth in the first two decades of the present century – after 2020 a yearly growth rate of 1 percent in the EU-15, Northern America and Japan[22] leading to the alternative simulation B1, shown in Appendix B.

Studies from the beginning of the 21st century – e.g. L.J. Kotlikoff et al. [2001] for the US and the EU Economic Policy Committee in its 'Lisbon scenario' [2000]) – assume a productivity growth in the first half of the current century of only 1 percent annually, leading to the alternative simulation B2, shown in Appendix B. Note that these are forecasts of a future remarkably and significantly worse than developed countries have experienced since a long time.
Furthermore, it is an even heroic assumption as well that productivity rates will converge to either 1¾ percent, 1 percent or whatever figure in all countries in the coming decades, as growth rates of real GDP per person employed differed widely among nations and decades in the last thirty years, e.g. over the 1990's ranging

---

21 The assumption of a convergence of labour productivity towards a (lower) 1,7 percent to 1,8 percent annually is found in the Progress Report of the EU Economic Policy Committee [2000] and in its report on budgetary challenges [2001]. OECD [2000a] and Dang et al. [2001] maintain productivity growth to converge towards an annual 1¾ percent as from between 2020 and 2030. The INGENUE team [2001] is also rather optimistic assuming 2 percent productivity growth in Northern America, and by a long-run convergence process in the medium, long and very long term all countries in the world reach the American level and grow at the same rate. For the Netherlands: CPB [2000] 1¾ percent and D.P. Broer [2001] 2 percent.

22 Decomposing the growth of output per worker in factor productivity (technology) and capital-labour substitution (capital deepening) reveals us that in Europe in the last two and a half decades of output growth (viz. 2¼ to 2½ percent) a part 1¼ to 1½ percent was due to technological advance and a part of 1 percent was due to capital deepening (B. Bosworth [1996]). It seems reasonable, therefore, to assume a yearly growth rate of average production per worker of 2 percent (in the period 2000-2020), which can be decomposed in 1 percent in respect of technology and another 1 percent in respect of capital deepening. After 2020 – when a) capital deepening is assumed to come to an end, b) the work force is aging further and c) the shift from the industrial sector with higher productivity growth to the service sector with lower productivity growth continues – a modest 1 per cent growth rate (technology) is presupposed. This is a conservative estimate (OECD/D. Turner et al. [1998] presuppose an annual 1.4 percent). The Economic Policy Committee [2000] in its 'Lisbon scenario' supposes productivity growth in European countries to converge to that expected for the US, a slight 1 percent on average in the first half of the 21st century. As a consequence a slowdown in economic development results. On the other hand, labour scarcity may induce a more rapid rate of technological innovation.

from 0.8 percent for the Netherlands to 3.2 percent for Ireland (EU-15 1.8 percent, the US 1.7 percent and Japan 1.3 percent)[23].

A slowdown in labour force growth (or even a decline) and a slowdown in productivity growth will lead to a lower rate of economic growth than the European economies, the US and Japan have experienced over an extended period of time.
Further adverse developments can arise. We can imagine that participation rates hardly increase. The shrinkage of the labour force and a higher wage level (due to labour scarcity) lead to reduced savings and can induce part of the capital stock becoming obsolete, which is harmful for the competitiveness of the economy. That will impede product and process innovation and investments, leading to falling productivity. Production is increasingly relocated abroad[24]. A downward spiral develops with lower consumption, saving, investment and employment. The old-age income system can no longer be sustained.
A worst case simulation B3 with a negative 1 percent annual growth till 2010, zero growth during the decade 2010-2020 and a following recovery by 1 percent growth over the period 2020-2050 is shown in Appendix B.

To the extent that the increase of wages, however, can be compensated by productivity growth (with remaining constant investment and correspondingly high capital deepening), such negative distortionary effects will be absent. If this can be assumed to be the case, the economy's competitive position does not suffer from a higher (nominal) wage level. Domestic consumption, saving and investment are growing steadily. Moreover, an expanding world economy will prevent interest rates to decline. The living standard of all citizens, workers and the elderly, in this favourable scenario stabilizes at a high level.
A larger effective labour supply due to higher participation will lead to lower wage increases and, hence, less incentives to substitute capital for labour and less productivity growth. On the other hand, lower wage increases may stimulate product and production process innovation, leading to higher investment and productivity growth. The net effect is ambiguous. We heroically assume that employment growth does not affect per worker productivity. Or, in other words, no trade-off exists between employing new less experienced workers and productivity growth.

---

23 Cf J. Elmeskow and S. Scarpetta [2000]. For the EU-15 area as a whole and Japan productivity rates were lower in the 1990's compared with the previous two decades, but the trend was reversed in the US and in some smaller EU-countries.

24 The economic performance of many modern economies is heavily conditioned by the (degree of) openness of the economy and the world globalisation. This makes these economies interdependent and also vulnerable. As a result independent and autonomous decision-making in respect of monetary and fiscal policy (in the first place), but e.g. also in respect of labour market, social and pension policy are severely constrained.

4.1.6 Decomposition

Growth in the production of per capita GDP can be decomposed in i) the demographic component, i.e. the share of the working age population in the total population, ii) the participation ratio, the ratio of employed persons to the working age population and iii) labour productivity, defined as GDP per person employed.

During the 1990's demography had only a minor effect on the growth of per capita GDP in the OECD-countries, apart from Korea and Ireland. For the EU-15 the demographic effect was slightly negative. Demography will be of more relevance from 2020 onwards in the EU-15 and Japan as the share of older people in the total population grows. In the EU-15 the share of employed persons in the total population in the coming two decades will rise from 0.42 to 0.46, mainly as the result of an increasing participation rate. After 2020/2025 the size of the labour force will contribute virtually nothing or even negatively to the growth of welfare. The share of employed persons in the total population will decrease to 0.39 by 2050.

Decreased labour force participation contributed negatively to economic growth during the 1990's in the EU-15, the Netherlands being a marked exception. Labour productivity growth, hence, accounted for more than GDP per capita growth.

Concluding, rising labour productivity will be the main contributor over the first two decades of the current century; after 2020 it will be the only contributing factor.

4.2 Scenarios of the demographic transition in developing countries

The less developed countries differ from the EU-15, Northern America and Japan in that they are aging not until the second half of the 21st century, but they age faster. Nonetheless they remain young during the 21st century. Less developed countries continue to be characterized by a relatively high supply of labour and a relatively low supply of capital. Hence, the rate of return on capital in many developing countries may be higher than in the developed world and wages will be lower.

4.2.1 Demographic dividend

When fertility rates decline, the working age population will grow at least in relative terms. Countries with a large working age population have an opportunity to capitalize on the 'demographic dividend', which can help to produce a sustained period of economic growth as extra labour can be introduced into the economy.

The demographic dividend is delivered through increased labour supply, savings and human capital (technology). Falling fertility rates are lowering the number of

dependent youngsters to the non-dependents of 18 to 60 years of age. Also women are more likely to enter the labour force as family size declines. Provided the labour market can absorb the larger number of workers, per capita national product grows.
The working population tends to consume less than it generates, particularly those between 40 and 60 years old (instead it saves predominantly for retirement purposes), unlike the young and the elderly. Hence, the demographic transition encourages the growth of savings, leading to higher investments and higher economic growth.
The demographic transition begins with falling mortality rates, resulting in a population living longer, healthier and leading to considerable changes in the way people live. Investments in human capital are stimulated and people are thus becoming more valuable assets. The demographic transition has significant effects on investing in education and occupational training, effects which are the least tangible, but the most significant and far-reaching.

The capture of the demographic dividend can be impeded by labour market rigidities and by a negative impact of population growth on the amount of capital per worker, i.e. the capital intensity, thereby lowering growth of welfare.
Economic development is not an automatic process; the demographic dividend has to be earned. Without appropriate policy measures countries with a large, young working age population at best will miss an opportunity to secure high economic growth, as today's undereducated youth will become tomorrow's underemployed workers. At worst, they will face rising and massive unemployment, high crime rates, political instability and economic and social disaster.

Russia and the other former Sowjet Republics as well simultaneously show early and profound aging, which can be threatening to the proper functioning of their economies. Russia's population will fall from 146 million in 2000 to 118.2 million by 2050. Although countries such as Japan show the same demographic pattern, they have had the benefit of a large baby boom generation contributing to high economic growth, yielding them a better starting position to cope with the demographic transition to an older population. Unfortunately the former Sowjet republics and other Eastern European countries do not have such dividend.

4.2.2 Alternative scenarios

For the less developed countries in Asia and Latin America and the smaller Eastern European countries apart from the present productivity scenario of 1¾ percent two more optimistic scenarios with growth rates, viz. 3½ percent and 2½ percent annually are considered. Unfortunately for the former Sowjet Republics and the majority of African countries as an alternative to the 1¾ percent productivity growth scenario a less optimistic scenario of zero percent growth rate seems more likely. Distinguished categories of less developed countries are termed more happy, (normal) happy and less happy countries respectively. In respect of labour force participation arbitrarily slight increases are supposed to take place. The findings of the alternatively more and less optimistic growth scenarios are shown in Appendix B, Table B4.

The vast majority of the world's population is still without some form of income security in old age. Only around 40 percent of the world's working population and a 30 percent of the elderly are covered by a formal pension scheme. Virtually the whole population in developing countries is without formal arrangements for old age, rather relying on informal or intra-family means of support. In many developing countries the situation of the elderly has deteriorated. Modernization and simultaneous economic crises are detrimental to the economic and social status of the aged as they undermine the capacity of communities and families to support the elderly and the willingness or commitment to meet traditional obligations. Elderly people without the support of extended families belong to the poorest groups in society. In particular, the position of elderly widows is highly vulnerable. With changing economic, social and political conditions the intergenerational support mechanisms weaken, including the remittance economy, which gives rural households shares of migrants' income.

Finally, the terms working age, non-working age, labour force participation, aging burden indicate the Western origins of the terminology. In most developing countries children start work on the land at young ages and elders work till they no longer can do so. Conversely, elderly cost less than children. The term dependency rate is largely fictitious as it is normal to work till death.
Pension systems or public assistance do not exist – or only for small urban elites – and when health care costs are high, only few appear in hospitals. It can be concluded, therefore, that a serious aging problem, let alone an aging burden do not exist in developing countries for many decades ahead. The most far-reaching scenario implies no aging at all.

4.3 Can the world population grow older comfortably?

The future of old age and pension systems in the EU-15 is nowadays a widely discussed topic. Unfortunately, the debate compared to that in the US can be qualified as rather poor. An exception can be made for the Netherlands, where The Netherlands Bureau for Economic Policy Analysis (CPB) has published several excellent studies on this subject. In the US many studies were and are devoted to the so-called pension crisis, which has resulted in a large and rich literature, though the scale of the problems in the US is considerably smaller than in many European countries. The question necessarily is raised whether a serious crisis will arise in the major continental European countries in the coming decades or, in other words, are the (Western) more developed countries rich enough to sustain an older population affordably?
In the present and following chapters we make clear that no major difficulties exist or, if any, that they can adequately be overcome on a macro-level, but that serious budgetary problems may arise on a micro and meso-level.

4.3.1 Basic economics

The total output of the economy is measured by gross domestic product (GDP) and can be decomposed in consumption expenditures (CE), investments (I) and the surplus/shortage on the current account of the balance of payments. Adjusted for price movements they are called real GDP, real CE and real I. Per capita CE is commonly used as a measure of personal welfare.

The consumption expenditures are quite a stable proportion of GDP in the long run. Estimates of GDP and GDP growth are also estimates of CE and CE growth and hence of the growth of personal welfare, though the value of consumption of leisure time should also be taken into account.

To demonstrate whether the economies of the aging developed countries have the prospective resources to permit (early) retirement, expanded health care and expanded other types of government expenditures, the focus in the present analysis is on the average producer and the average consumer. Three age groups are distinguished. This is a marked simplification of reality – to overcome the frustrating sterility that everything depends on every thing else –, thereby disregarding the dynamic economics on a meso or intermediate level and at a micro or personal level. An explanation in more detail of the methodology used is given in Appendix A.

Table 3A presents evidence on national welfare, measured by per capita consumptional expenditures, in developed countries – the EU-15, the US, Canada and Japan – by 2020 and 2050. The base year 2000 has index 100. To measure the aging burden per capita welfare under the projected age distribution as well as under the unchanged age structure in the base year are shown. Similar information in respect of Russia, the smaller Eastern European countries and a selection of developing countries from Asia, Latin America and Africa are presented in Table 3B.

4.3.2 Aging and welfare in the 21st century

The case of the EU-15 (first row in Table 3A) is discussed now in more detail for explanatory purposes. Under the assumptions made on labour force participation and productivity growth, total production in the EU-area makes possible an average per capita consumption by 2020 of 144.7 for all people over 20 years of age, with index 100 in the year 2000 for the group aged 20-64 years and index 80 for the 65^{+}-population. Per capita consumption amounts to 72.35 for the under-twenties (index 50 in the year 2000).

Developed countries

Consumption of the working age population in the EU-15 thus rises in the period 2000 to 2020 by 44.7 percent and the consumption of the 65^{+}-population by an impressive 80.9 percent (from index 80 in 2000 to index 144.7 in 2020).

Note that there is even room for a further increase of consumption. The EU-15, the US and Japan generate balance of payments surpluses of 2 à 3 percent GDP up to

Table 3A. Welfare in more developed countries, EU-15, US Canada and Japan in the years 2020 and 2050 (indexes; the year 2000: 100), assuming 1¾ percent yearly production growth and some increase in the labour force participation rate (in 2050 ≤ 0.78 and 0.78), for an aging population and an unchanged (non-aging) population

Year	2020		2050		2050	
	Aging	Non-aging	Aging	Non-aging	Aging	Non-aging
Country			(partic. ratio ≤ 0.78)		(partic. ratio = 0.78)	
(1)	(2)	(3)	(4)	(5)	(6)	(7)
EU-15	**144.7**	**151.0**	**211.2**	**254.0**	**219.7**	**264.2**
Belgium	146.7	152.3	220.5	256.3	245.7	285.5
France	142.8	148.7	219.1	250.2	234.1	267.3
Germany	138.8	146.5	205.8	246.6	214.1	256.4
Italy	147.7	155.6	198.3	261.1	230.8	304.8
Netherlands	141.7	151.1	215.0	254.2	217.8	257.5
Spain	149.2	153.5	191.4	258.3	210.3	283.8
Sweden	133.8	142.0	213.0	238.9	equal (4)	equal (5)
UK	139.9	143.2	212.0	240.9	equal (4)	equal (5)
Other world						
US	133.1	133.9	209.1	233.7	equal (4)	equal (5)
Canada	135.2	141.2	205.2	237.7	equal (4)	equal (5)
Japan	120.4	138.4	178.9	233.0	equal (4)	equal (5)

Table 3B. **Welfare in Eastern Europe and less developed countries in the years 2020 and 2050 (indexes; the year 2000: 100), assuming 1¾ percent yearly production growth and a slight increase in the labour force participation rate (in 2050 ≤ 0.78 and 078) for an aging population and an unchanged (non-aging) population**

Year	2020		2050		2050	
	Aging	Non-aging	Aging	Non-aging	Aging	Non-aging
			(partic. ratio ≤ 0.78)		(partic. ratio = 0.78)	
Country						
(1)	(2)	(3)	(4)	(5)	(6)	(7)
Eastern Europe						
Russia	148.5	149.4	216.6	251.4	225.2	261.4
Ukraine	149.3	149,2	220,8	251,0	229.7	261.1
Poland	148.9	151.6	210.3	255.1	218.7	265.3
Czech Republic	131.0	139.3	178.7	234.4	131.0	228.5
Romania	148.8	149.3	207.7	251.2	216.0	261.2
Hungary	156.1	162.3	222.2	273.2	247.5	304.4
Other world						
China	150.9	150.3	219.7	291.1	228.5	303.7
India	162.0	150.7	260.1	253.6	270.5	263.7
Pakistan	176.3	150.8	299.0	253.7	311.0	263.8
Indonesia	156.1	150.7	243.2	253.7	252.9	263.8
Iran	177.4	150.7	265.0	253.6	275.6	263.7
Turkey	162.0	150.5	235.7	253.2	245.1	263.3
Brazil	157.4	150.6	236.4	253.4	245.1	263.5
Mexico	162.4	150.8	249.0	253.7	259.0	263.8
Argentina	153.1	149.7	245.3	251.9	255.1	262.0
Egypt	164.7	150.8	263.9	253.8	274.4	264.0
Nigeria	158.4	151.0	302.8	254.1	315.0	264.3
Kenya	182.9	151.0	313.4	254.1	326.0	264.3
South Africa	154.0	150.7	267.0	253.5	277.6	263.7

2025, thus building up a stock of net foreign assets. From the returns of it the import of consumer goods can be paid. Secondly, a further welfare growth can be achieved by an increased capital intensity, leading to higher production per worker and rising wage rate, but also lower capital revenues. It must be emphasized again that the aforementioned welfare gains of 44.7 percent and 80.9 percent over the first two decades of the 21st century critically depend on a broad range of successful policy measures stimulating the economy (chapter 6).

In a demographically unchanged population (no aging from 2000 onwards) per capita consumption would be 151.0 for all people over 20 years of age instead of 144.7. The difference between the indexes 151 and 144.7, hence, can be considered as the consumption sacrifice or the amount of consumptional expenditures forgone by the younger population groups in favour of the elderly. The difference of 6.3 (index 151 minus index 144.7) can be regarded as the increased tax necessary to support a larger number of non-producing elders. Or, in other words, welfare in 2020 is 4.2 percent lower than otherwise without aging would have been the case.
Between 2020 and 2050 according to rather optimistic assumptions per capita consumption increases with about 1.3 percent annually, leading to a consumption index 211.2 by 2050 (the year 2020: 144.7). In the non-aging environment the consumption index would be 254.0. The difference, amounting to 42.8 (index 254 minus index 211.2), being the consumption sacrifice should not be ignored but also should not be considered as dramatic. Welfare in the EU-15 by 2050 relative to 2000 is 16.8 percent lower that would have been the case without aging.
Differences exist among EU-15 member states. Most EU-countries can gain from a substantial increase in the participation ratio in the coming decades. In Sweden and the UK with already relatively high labour participation in 2000 the increase in per capita consumption by 2020 and 2050 is less than in other countries.

The same holds for the US, Canada and Japan. There is no labour force participation dividend that can be reaped.

Developing countries and transitional economies

Though the less developed countries are aging faster than most other parts of the world, there is far from an aging problem. The difference is that the main cause of aging in developing countries is a fall in the birth rate rather than an increase in the number of (old) people over 60. Hence, in many developing countries the working age population is growing in absolute and relative terms (relative to the number aged 0-19 and 65 and over), yielding them a demographic bonus of a young and potentially healthy and well-educated work force. Per capita welfare in the aging environment in virtually all developing countries over the first half of the 21st century can be higher compared with the scenario of an unchanged age structure of their population. The major exception is China by the year 2050 due to effective birth control policies.
Russia and the smaller Eastern European countries are fastly aging. Hungary can benefit from an initial low labour force participation, opposed to the Czech

Republic with a labour participation as high as 0.80 by 2000, hitting the ceiling. The other transitional economies are in an intermediate position.

4.3.3 Strain on political, social and economic systems

The prospective production capacity in the EU-15 member states, thus, enables consumptional expenditures to rise from 100 in 2000 to 144.7 by 2020 and further to 211.2 by 2050 (2000: 100). We may conclude therefore that the resources to finance the expanded demand of workers and pensioners for e.g. high-quality medical services, education, consumer durables, housing, etc, etc will be abundant. There is room for a further reduction of the length of the yearly working time or to retire earlier (if one prefers). Real consumption of the working age population by 2020 is 51.0 percent higher before (increased) tax and 44.7 percent higher after tax. Or, in other words, after tax paying standards of living of workers and pensioners are substantially higher than they are today. The tax increase, thus, is economically feasible.

Nonetheless, in the more developed countries it may occur that the growth in the size of the older population will indeed strain political, social and economic systems.

Allegedly a higher tax or contribution level is not (or hardly) feasible from a psychological or political point of view. Arguing that the welfare of individuals after the tax increase is still 44.7 percent higher than it is today and much higher than people had a generation ago, will probably not persuade them to accept the tax increase and will not take away their misgivings to be overtaxed and exploited. But this is by no means certain. Much depends on the rate at which non-working people at date enter the labour force, the growth of productivity, the effects of economic restructuring and above all, our success in developing effective policies for intergenerational integration.

Secondly, the share of income destined for old-age purposes can increase as personal income rises.

Concluding

Given the psychological and political strains the search for a system of financing retirement income and health care at old age is the search for a system that can be accepted wholeheartedly by all irrespective (up to a certain extent) the height of the tax. All individuals under that system are required when young to set aside a quarter to a third of their income (in a collective or personal account or otherwise) to use for old-age income purposes, health and long-term care included. Thereby individuals create a resource base of their own. Time bombs will not explode nor political explosions will occur in 2010, in 2040 or in any other year. This issue is pursued in chapter 5.

4.3.4 Alternative productivity growth rates

Table 4 below shows the consumption level of the adult population in 2020 (the year 2000: 100) with assumed increased labour force participation rates in all countries under study and under different growth rates of production per worker, 0 percent, 1¾ percent (also shown in Tables 3A and 3B) and 2½ percent respectively. Table 4A presents evidence for the more developed countries and Table 4B for the transitional economies and a selection of less developed countries (both year 2020).

In column (2) of Table 4A and Table 4B the effect on welfare of a higher participation ratio (for the EU-15 rising from 0.69 to 0.75) combined with a zero growth of productivity is shown. Columns (3) to (5) give evidence of the welfare-gain of alternative productivity growth rates with (constant) participation at the higher level.

Developed countries

With zero growth rate of production per worker for the EU-15 as a whole there remains a slight increase in welfare of 2.3 percent in 2020 relative to 2000, due to the fact that labour force participation is assumed to rise from 0.69 in 2000 to 0.75 in 2020[25]. Welfare is decreasing with some percentage points in Germany and Sweden and slightly more than one percentage point in the UK. Welfare decreases are more substantial in the US, Canada and Japan, where participation rates were already high at the turn of the century and could hardly be higher.

Only with an unchanged labour force participation rate (of 0.69) as in the baseline year 2000 and a zero growth rate of production per worker, the consumption level of the adult population in the EU-15 is decreasing from 100 in 2000 to 94.1 in 2020, which seems (very) serious but not utterly dramatic as nobody will starve. With increased labour force participation from 0.69 to 0.75 there is a slight (almost negligible) rise in welfare of 2.3 percent in the EU-15 over the first two decades of the current century. In other words, if the EU-15 succeeds only partly in raising employment to US levels (with a participation ratio of 0.78 in 2000), there would be no serious aging problem. Per capita welfare at least remains constant over the coming decades.

In the other two productivity growth scenarios (1¾ percent and 2½ percent annual growth respectively), however, the standard of living not only can be maintained, but there is ample scope for a further increase in welfare, ranging from 144.7 to a formidable 167.6 by 2020. Note however that productivity growth hampers, when the economy is short of skilled labour.

25 The right amount of labour market reform measures, resulting in a participation rate of 0.73 by 2020 (and 0.84 by 2050!, not shown in the Table) with no productivity growth can on its own compensate for the adverse effects of population aging on welfare. On the other hand, a slight 0.3 percent productivity growth with unchanged labour force participation suffices to maintain welfare on the year 2000 level.

Table 4A. Consumption level of the 20⁺- population in 2020 under alternative growth rates of production per worker (EU-15, US, Canada and Japan; increased labour force participation; year 2000: 100)

	Growth rate of production per worker (percent)			
	0	0	1¾	2½
Country	(unchanged partic.)	(	← higher participation →	)
(1)	(2)	(3)	(4)	(5)
EU-15	**94.1**	**102.3**	**144.7**	**167.6**
Belgium	94.5	103.7	146.7	169,9
France	94.2	101.0	142.8	165.4
Germany	93.0	98.1	138.8	160.8
Italy	93.0	104.4	147.7	171.0
Netherlands	92.3	100.2	141.7	164.1
Spain	95.4	105.5	149.2	172.8
Sweden	93.9	96.1	133.8	157.5
UK	96.0	98.9	139.9	162.0
Other world				
US	94.4	94.0	133.1	154.1
Canada	94.3	95.5	135.2	156.6
Japan	85.3	85.1	120.4	139.5

Table 4B. Consumption level of the 20⁺- population in 2020 under alternative growth rates of production per worker (Eastern Europe and less developed countries; modest increase in labour force participation; year 2000: 100)

	Growth rate of production per worker (percent)			
	0	0	1¾	2½
Country	(unchanged partic.)	(	← higher participation →	)
(1)	(2)	(3)	(4)	(5)
Eastern Europe				
Russia	97.8	104.7	148.5	171.6
Ukraine	98.5	105.5	149.3	173.0
Poland	96.8	105.3	148.9	172.5
Czech Republic	92.6	92.6	131.0	151.7
Romania	98.2	105.2	148.8	172.3
Hungary	95.0	110.8	156.1	181.6
Other world				
China	99.6	106.7	150.9	174.8
India	106.9	114.5	162.0	187.6
Pakistan	116.3	124.6	176.3	204.2
Indonesia	103.4	110.8	156.8	181.6
Iran	117.0	125.4	177.4	205.4
Turkey	106.9	114.5	162.0	187.6
Brazil	103.9	111.3	157.4	182.4
Mexico	107.1	114.8	162.4	188.1
Argentina	101.0	108.2	153.1	177.4
Egypt	108.7	116.4	164.7	190.8
Nigeria	104.5	112.0	158.4	183.5
Kenya	120.7	129.3	182.9	211.9
South Africa	101.6	108.9	154.0	178.4

Developing countries

The developing countries in all productivity growth scenarios fare better than the developed countries in relative terms. Growth rates of GDP and welfare in the less developed countries are higher over the first two decades of the 21st century due to their larger growing working age population.

Concluding

Productivity growth allows per capita consumption of all age groups to rise throughout the period of demographic transition. Nobody has to 'sacrifice'. Production will be sufficient to substantially increase the per capita consumption of all age groups. All age groups in 2020 are on average better off – and in 2050 much better off – than in 2000. Hence, the burden of a larger number of retirees should be borne rather easily.
But this is not the whole story. It appears difficult to construct adequate financial arrangements – and satisfactory for all –, to implement the distribution of total GDP to younger and older generations.

4.3.5 Required productivity growth to maintain welfare

We can also reverse the question and examine which yearly growth rate of labour productivity is necessary to offset the negative impact of population aging on living standards or average per capita consumption in 2020. Subsequently the question is answered which level of productivity growth is necessary to achieve 15 percent, 30 percent or 60 percent growth of average per capita consumption over the time period 2000-2020. Evidence is presented in Table 5A for the more developed countries and in Table 5B for the transitional economies and the less developed countries.

It turns out that a modest rate of technological progress is (necessary and) sufficient to offset the adverse consequences of aging on welfare and the consumption level. With increased labour force participation of the working age population a growth rate of average production per worker of -0.11 percent in the EU-15 suffices to keep welfare at a constant level[26]. Or, in other words, even a slowdown of the yearly productivity growth rate to 0.11 percent, combined with a higher labour force participation guarantees an equal welfare level in the EU-15 by 2020 as in the year 2000. Note that the productivity growth in the last two decades of the 20th century amounted to about 2½ percent. Furthermore, a growth rate of production per worker of zero necessitates the labour force participation ratio to rise from 0.69 to 0.73 to offset any detrimental effect of population aging on welfare.

---

26 It can make a difference for workers' perception of bearing the pension burden in an aging population whether GDP growth is reached by productivity growth with a constant or even smaller labour force or by expanding the working population. In the former case higher gross wages and higher contribution rates will result than in the latter case with higher employment and slower productivity growth.

Table 5A. Growth rate of production per worker (percentage) required to achieve zero percent, 15 percent, 30 percent or 60 percent higher level of consumption of the 20$^+$-population in 2020 (EU-15, US, Canada and Japan; increased labour force participation)

	Desired growth of consumption level from 2000 to 2020 (percent)				
	0	**0**	**15**	**30**	**60**
Country	(unchanged partic.)	(	← higher participation →		)
(1)	(2)	(3)	(4)	(5)	(6)
EU-15	**0.31**	**-0.11**	**0.59**	**1.21**	**2.26**
Belgium	0.18	-0.28	0.42	1.04	2.09
France	0.30	-0.04	0.66	1.27	2.33
Germany	0.36	0.09	0.80	1.42	2.47
Italy	0.36	-0.21	0.49	1.10	2.16
Netherlands	0.40	-0.01	0.83	1.45	2.51
Spain	0.24	-0.27	0.43	1.05	2.11
Sweden	0.32	0.20	0.90	1.52	2.58
UK	0.21	0.06	0.76	1.38	2.44
Other world					
US	0.29	0.31	1.01	1.63	2.69
Canada	0.29	0.23	0.93	1.55	2.61
Japan	0.80	0.81	1.52	2.14	3.21

Table 5B. Growth rate of production per worker (percentage) required to achieve zero percent, 15 percent, 30 percent or 60 percent higher level of consumption of the 20^{+}-population in 2020 (Eastern Europe and less developed countries; modest increase in labour force participation)

	Desired growth of consumption level from 2000 to 2020 (percent)				
	0	0	15	30	60
	(unchanged partic.)	(	← higher participation →		)
Country					
(1)	(2)	(3)	(4)	(5)	(6)
Eastern Europe					
Russia	0.11	-0.23	0.47	1.09	2.14
Ukraine	0.08	-0.27	0.43	1.05	2.05
Poland	0.16	-0.26	0.44	1.06	2.12
Czech Republic	0.39	0.39	1.09	1.71	2.77
Romania	0.09	-0.25	0.45	1.07	2.12
Hungary	0.26	-0.51	0.19	0.80	1.85
Other world					
China	0.02	-0.32	0.38	0.99	2.05
India	-0.33	-0.67	0.02	0.64	1.69
Pakistan	-0.75	-1.09	-0.40	0.21	1.26
Indonesia	-0.17	-0.51	0.19	0.80	1.85
Iran	-0.78	-1.12	-0.43	0.18	1.23
Turkey	-0.33	-0.68	0.02	0.64	1.69
Brazil	-0.19	-0.53	0.16	0.78	1.83
Mexico	-0.34	-0.69	0.01	0.63	1.68
Argentina	-0.05	-0.40	0.30	0.92	1.97
Egypt	-0.41	-0.76	0.06	0.55	1.60
Nigeria	-0.22	-0.56	0.13	0.75	1.80
Kenya	-0.94	-1.28	-0.59	0.03	1.07
South Africa	-0.88	-0.42	0.27	0.89	1.94

On the other hand, if overall participation rates were to remain constant, the working population of the EU-15 needs to be almost 6.5 percent more productive in the year 2020 relative to 2000 – or an annual productivity growth rate of 0.31 percentage points – if it is to produce the same per capita quantity of goods and services.
Alternative policy measures to increase labour force participation and to stimulate immigration necessary to maintain per capita welfare are dealt with in paragraphs 6.3.2 and 6.3.7.

Marked differences exist between EU-15 member states. The lowest productivity growth rates are needed in Belgium and the UK (0.18 percent and 0.21 percent respectively) and the highest growth rates are required in the Netherlands, Germany and Italy (from 0.36 percent to 0.40 percent). In Japan an annual 0.8 percent growth rate of productivity is necessary to guarantee the same welfare level in 2020 as in 2000. Or, in other words, in Japan fifty percent or more of the average long-term productivity growth will be 'eaten up' by the changing age structure of its population. The US and Canada take on an intermediate position, both with 0.29 percentage annual growth rate necessary to maintain the per capita consumption level[27].

Concluding

As pointed out in the preceding paragraph, the adverse effects of an older age structure in the EU-15 countries are to a large extent compensated for by the increase in labour force participation. Further welfare growth can only be achieved 0.59 percent annually combined with a higher labour force participation results in by continuing productivity growth. A rather modest increase in productivity of a growth of per capita consumption in 2020 of 15 percent relative to the year 2000. A moderate yearly productivity growth of 1.22 percent leads to a welfare increase of 30 percent in 2020.

From Table 4A it follows that in EU-15 a yearly growth rate of labour productivity ranging between 1 percent and 2½ percent combined with increased labour force participation, gives rise to considerable welfare increases in the year 2020 vis-à-vis the year 2000, varying between 24.8 percent and 67.6 percent. Welfare increases in Belgium, Italy and Spain are among the highest, as those countries reap their labour participation dividend. High annual productivity rates are required, if we are to sustain the rates of welfare growth we were accustomed to during extended periods in the second half of the 20th century, 3 to 4 percent on an annual basis. To achieve 60 percent or more welfare growth over the period 2000-2020 (equivalent to 2.4 percent per annum), annual productivity growth rates

27 Similarly D.M. Cutler et al. [1990], '... even a 0.2 percentage point increase in annual productivity growth between 1990 and 2040 would offset the decrease in per capita consumption as a result of rising dependency burdens over that period [...], there is little evidence for the more pessimistic view of demographic change.'

of at least 2.26 percent in the EU-15, 2.69 percent in the US and 3.21 percent in Japan are needed.

The significance of productivity growth in the transitional economies is the same as in the EU-15 countries. In developing countries the productivity growth rates necessary for a particular increase of welfare are less than in the aging developed societies due to the relatively larger size of their working age population.

4.4 Spending on welfare and intergenerational ethics

A continuing growth of spending on 'welfare' as part of total spending will, we believe, be more easily borne by citizens, at least from a psychological point of view and up from a certain level, when it is private and not public and when it is voluntary and not mandatory. Or, in other words, individuals are willing and able to take more responsibility on themselves in the field of pension provision and health care, as their income and wealth increase. Secondly, funding will also increasingly finance the provision of welfare services, particularly health care and other long-term care, as most of the consumption of those services takes place during old age. As such they can be compared with pension income provisions.
The major growth, thus, will be in privately rather than in publicly financed categories of welfare expenditures. This will almost inevitably lead to a growing inequality in levels of consumption of welfare goods; the redistributive impact will change. The basic question arises where, when and for whom the disadvantages of inter- and intragenerational solidarity outweigh the advantages. Under which conditions solidarity is no longer a benefit, but a burden?
At the same time also a reallocation of labour from the more productive industrial sector to the less productive sector of (care) services takes place, contributing to a lower growth rate of GDP, which will burden current solidarity.

Spending on 'welfare' as a share of national income will continue to rise over the 21st century and to suggest this is 'something we can not afford' seems to be a statement with little economic and historical understanding. In a period where real per capita income continues to increase for the whole population, it is illogical to infer that some – viz. the older – part of the population inevitably must suffer a slowing down or even a decrease in income. We certainly can wish and decide to do that, but scarcity of resources will not bring us to that type of inference, though other values and convictions certainly can. Declaring that the more developed countries are facing a lost half-century is unnecessarily creating a dismal atmosphere.

Towards a new intergenerational contract

Nonetheless, it seems necessary that the (concept of the) intergenerational solidarity of the 20th century has to be replaced by other forms of cultural integration towards a new intergenerational contract, a new commitment to justice.

The internal social cohesion of a society stands or falls by the (perceived) balance between groups of population, particularly young and old cohorts[28].
It has been pointed out by R.W. Fogel that immaterial assets are becoming the dominant form of wealth in the future world, equalizing the distribution of spiritual resources may be helpful to create intergenerational ethics. Hence, intergenerational justice and equity become a pressing issue[29].

Aging is the result of a process of continuous and increasing civilization during the last one and half century in the developed world – the process started with ameliorated sanitary and housing conditions, followed by a broad supply of medical and welfare and old-age social security services, giving birth to the welfare state of the 20th century – and, hence, should not be considered as a problem. Its fiscal and economic implications, nonetheless, may be such that we cannot permit ourselves doing nothing.

4.4.1 Concluding observations

Real per capita output in Western countries doubled between 1960 and 1995 and would double again between 1995 and 2030 to 2035. It can be concluded that without doubt we can afford to grow older. We in the European countries (and elsewhere in the more developed world as well) are rich enough to sustain an old-age pension for a more numerous older population. A fortiori, it can be said that we are approaching saturation in the consumption of material goods, not only of necessities but of luxury goods as well, which were only science fiction or dreams during the first half of the 20th century[30].

It is (too) easy to forget how rapidly real incomes have grown over the 20th century, viz. about a sevenfold increase. At current trend growth rates GDP will double in real terms roughly every 30 to 35 years. As individuals and nations grow more affluent they tend to increase the share of total spending devoted to some commodities and reduce the share devoted to others. Food is a clear example of the first category. Outlays for health, education and provision for incomes in retirement, sickness/disability and unemployment will all increase their share as per capita national income rise. As individuals and nations continue to grow more

---

28 An European overview of the politics of old age and national case studies (Austria, France, Germany, Italy, Netherlands, Sweden, the UK, Hungary and the USA) are given by A. Walker and G. Naegele [1999].

29 Cf. R.W. Fogel [(winner Nobelprice in Economics 1993), *The fourth great awakening & the future of egalitarianism*, University of Chicago Press, Chicago, 2000] provides a list of spiritual resources. They are 1) 'a sense of purpose', 2) 'a vision of opportunity', 3) 'a sense of the mainstream of work and life', 4) 'a strong family ethic', 5) 'a sense of community', 6) 'a capacity to engage with diverse groups', 7) 'an ethic of benevolence', 8) 'a work ethic', 9) 'a sense of discipline', 10) 'the capacity to focus and concentrate one's efforts', 11) 'a capacity to resist the lure of hedonism', 12) 'a capacity for self-education', 13) 'a thirst for knowledge', 14) 'an appreciation for quality' and 15) 'self-esteem'.

30 In most western countries nowadays the poverty line is at a level of real income that was attained by only those in the highest 10 percent of the income distribution about 1900.

affluent it seems likely that they will wish to spend – and can afford to do so – more on pension income and health care. Hence, the share of expenditures for pension provisions and health care facilities in national income will grow further and as a result is not anything to be concerned about.

It is often said that the younger generation is no longer willing to give up such a large part of their income (a doubling or more) in the form of necessary contributions for the pension payments of the elderly[31]. Though welfare increases for all, it is argued that a relative deterioration will not be accepted, as the fiscal burden is already high.
This may be true, but we cannot be sure about this. We don't know whether a (by three to five percentage points) higher contribution level can not be borne by citizens nor do we know whether such an increase gives rise to labour market distortions with adverse effects on the proper functioning of the economy.

31 Some questions need to be answered. Have the youngsters reached some ceiling on their willingness and ability to finance pay-as-you-go based pensions? Can that ceiling be measured? Why they are unwilling to pay out of their much higher incomes the transfers to the retirees?

5 A paradox

As pointed out before the best guarantee that future pensions can be paid is a large volume of future national product[32]. A decline in the labour force and a slowing down of the productivity growth cause problems for any pension and welfare scheme to the extent that they induce a fall in output. The problem is solved to the extent this can be prevented or, preferably, the economy can be boosted.
But this is not the whole story. Budgetary and fiscal imbalances allegedly have harmful effects on the economy (inducing declines in output) and the income distribution. Furthermore, creating a situation that is unsustainable in the long run is highly unfair to the generations to come. The problems are solved to the extent that budgetary deficits can be eliminated.

5.1 The budgetary issue

Fiscal or budgetary sustainability is guaranteed if it is possible to keep up social security – particularly public pensions and publicly financed health and other long-term care – and other essential government expenditures at an level democratically and mutually agreed without having to raise taxes and other contributions more than the members of a society are able and willing to pay, taking into account that high tax rates are detrimental to the performance of the economy[33]. But we don't know for sure at what height of tax level distortionary effects (viz. reduced labour supply) arise.

5.1.1 The budgetary issue - public pensions

Raising the level of output, however, is not *per se* a solution to the fiscal pressures that result from tax financed public pensions and health care systems. It can be argued that not the size of future national product but the mechanism of *distributing* future national product among retired and non-retired, for a large part via the government budget, is the primary issue and this mechanism allegedly will create increasing difficulties.

---

32 Note that guarantees are in some way or other always virtual. In a pay-as-you-go scheme they are based on the strength of an implicit social contract between generations; under funding they are based on the ability of the economy always to yield an adequate return on financial assets. When, in a funded scheme, total monetary purchasing power or the demand for goods and services (largely) exceeds the value and amount of current output at prevailing prices, a general price inflation will bring them back into line.

33 The Netherlands Bureau of Economic Policy Analysis [CPB; 2000]: '... government policies are sustainable if current policies can be continued forever without the government running into financial problems; that are ... policies where tax rates are *constant* over time and expenditures grow by the general rate of productivity growth.' (pp. 38-39).

It has been observed by E.P. Davis [1998] that '... pay-as-you-go based pension systems pose broad problems to public finance and the wider economy, both now I It has been observed e.g. by Davis [1998] that '... pay-as-you-go based pension systems pose broad problems to public finance and the wider economy, both now and in the future.' The maturation of the social security pension systems is posing increasing difficulties.

Estimates of D. Roseveare et al. [1996] suggest that pension expenditures will rise by about 6 to 7 percent of GDP – from between 5 percent and 12 percent to between 15 percent and 20 percent – in the period 1990-2040 in Japan, Spain, Italy, Finland, Germany and Portugal. They showed less of an impact – rising from less than 5 percent to 8 percent of GDP – in the US and Canada. The UK stabilizes at 5 percent and Ireland notably shows a decline in pension costs[34]. Unchanged contribution rates clearly will lead to sizable public sector deficits and the negative budgetary impact will worsen if the deficits are accompanied by slower economic growth.

A recent study (October 2001) of the EU Economic Policy Commission[35] shows that public pension expenditures – including most public income replacement revenues to people aged 55 and over, e.g. disability, early retirement and survivors pensions – in the EU-15 rise from 10.4 percent of GDP in 2000 by 3.2 percentage points to 13.6 percent in 2040 (peak level) and 13.3 percent by 2050. The starting position in 2000 ranges from 5.5 percent of GDP in the UK via 7.9 percent in the Netherlands to 11.8 percent in Germany, 12.2 percent in France and 13.8 percent in Italy. The UK is the only member state to project a decrease in public pension

---

34 It is important to note that wide differences exist in projections of (trends of) pension costs between e.g. D. Franco & T. Munzi [1996], D. Roseveare et al. [1996] and S.K. Chand & A. Jaeger [1996]. To give a few examples, in the Netherlands public pension costs as a percentage of GDP rise in the period 1995-2030 from 6.0 to 11.2 conform the study of D. Roseveare et al.; from Franco/Munzi we derive that the contribution rate in respect of the Dutch public pension plan rises only slowly from 11.0 percent in 1995 to 13.0 percent in 2030 (of contribution base). For Ireland pension expenditures (as a percentage of GDP) decline from 3.6 to 2.8 and contribution rates increase from 13.6 to 23.5 (percentage of contribution base), both in the period 1995-2030 according to the two first mentioned studies. Chand/Jaeger reveal for Italy a contribution gap of a minor 2.5 percentage points (of GDP) between the sustainable contribution rate (for the period 1995-2050) and the actual contribution rate in 1995; in Franco/Munzi pension expenditures stabilize from 8.2 in 1995 (via 7.6 in 2010) to 8.3 (percentage of GDP) in 20230, whereas Roseveare et al. present the (expected) increase in pension expenditures from 13.3 in 1995 to 21.4 in 2040 (percentage of GDP).

35 EU Economic Policy Committee [24-12-2001]. Remarkably the projections for public pension expenditures and health and long-term care were conducted in parallel with an exercise of the OECD (Dang, T.-T. et al., 2001). Old age pensions rise in the USA from 4.4 percent of GDP in 2000 to 6.2 percent by 2050; in Canada the increase is from 5.1 tot 10.9 percent and in Japan from 7.9 to 8.5 percent over the first half of the 21st century.
Note also that without increase in labour force participation and neglecting recently introduced reform measures pension expenditures in the EU-15 as a percentage of GDP will rise by more than 7 percentage points from 10.4 in 2000 to 17.6 in 2050 (European Committee [2001]).

spending by 1.1 percentage points. Relatively small increases of between 2 and 3 percent of GDP are projected in Italy and Sweden. Belgium (+ 3.7 percentage points), France (+ 4.0 percentage points), Germany (+ 5.0 percentage points) and the Netherlands (+ 6.2 percentage points) show average increases in the level of public pension spending. In Spain and Greece 7.9 and 12.2 percentage points project the largest increases respectively. In the so-called Lisbon-scenario – characterized by a higher employment rate – a 1.3 percentage points lower level of spending on public pensions results by 2050.
Concluding, the increased burden implied by population aging on public pension expenditures is significant, but not dramatic provided that vigorous and adequate policy measures are taken.

5.1.2 The budgetary issue - health and long-term care

A fortiori the health and long-term care sector is expanding profoundly, as the proportion of the very old (one of the biggest users of health care services) is expected to treble. People of advanced age spend on average 8 to 10 times more on their health than do people aged 20-60 years. Particularly health expenditures rise rapidly as the end of life approaches. Moreover, technical progress in the medical field is continually pushing up per capita health care spending the more, as the population gets older. Contribution rates to the statutory health insurance organizations tend to double or more in most more developed countries.

Expenditures on health care increased substantially in Europe over the second half of the last century: doubling as a share of GDP over the period 1960-1990. Not aging but factors like increased coverage, increased demand, technology driven supply and high medical price inflation were significant driving forces of the increase in health care expenditures.
The EU Economic Policy Commission's Report on budgetary challenges shows that the pure consequences of aging on public expenditures for health and long-term care over the next fifty years in the EU-15 rise from 6.6 percent of GDP in 2000 by 2.7 percentage points to 9.3 percent in 2050. The starting position in 2000 ranges from 5.5 percent of GDP in Italy via 7.2 percent in the Netherlands to 8.8 percent in Sweden. The increase in percentage points of GDP from 2000 to 2050 ranges between 2.1 (Italy), via 2.5 (France and the UK) to 3.8 in the Netherlands and 3.9 in Finland. In the Northern European countries and in the Netherlands the largest part of this increase takes place through increased public expenditures on long-term care rather than health care.

By far the largest part of the increase in expenditures in all member states over the next fifty years is due to increases in expenditures on the older age groups, particularly the over-eighties age group, who are more vulnerable to severe disabilities and require more health, long-term and social care. Apart from this demographic effect, the main contributor to rising health care costs is technological innovation, leading to costly new medical equipment (diagnosis and treatment) and pharmaceuticals.

Concluding

The impact of aging on public expenditures on health and long-term care is significant – and can have repercussions for fiscal sustainability and debt dynamics – but not necessarily dramatic. Without adequate policies the strain on public finance and its repercussions can be become serious.

As fiscal burdens in many countries are already high and further increases could be detrimental to the performance of the economy there is much concern about the fiscal sustainability of the population aging process[36]. Most of the simulated policy reforms – drastic cuts in benefits – and fiscal consolidation result in a sustained period of depressed per capita consumption of goods and services. Furthermore, it takes a long time for policy reforms to have significant macroeconomic impacts[37].

According to D. Miles [1997] the scope to increase general taxation to finance public pensions is limited due to serious distortions of higher taxes to economic activity. As a consequence in his view significant reductions in public pension schemes in Europe over the next 30 to 40 years seem likely. Note, however, that there is no clear idea of how high tax and contribution levels could be and at what heights distortionary economic impacts occur.

5.1.3 Aging, longevity and health care expenditures

The impact of population aging for health care expenditures may be profound, as elderly persons use health care services at a greater rate than younger persons. The over-eighties age group absorbs 8 to 10 times the per capita health care costs devoted to the under-sixties age group. Note that projections for health care spending including long-term care are considerably more uncertain than for pension expenditures.

Noteworthy evidence found by B.C. Spillman and J. Lubitz [2000] for the US is summarized below.

Cumulative health care expenditures (in 1966 US dollars) from the age of 65 years until death increase substantially with longevity, from about $ 31,000 for persons who die at the age of 65 to more than $ 200,000 for those who die at the age of 90 and further to about $ 400,000 for the small number of people dying at the age of 100 and over. Health care spending in the last two years of life increases slowly with the age of death, amounting from $ 46,000 per person to about $ 55,000 for those who die at the age of 95.

In the US the effect of longevity on expenditures for acute care differs from its effect on expenditures for long-term care. Acute care expenditures, principally for

36 Expressed i.a. by D. Franco and T. Munzi [European Commission, 1996], S.K. Chand and A. Jaeger [IMF, 1996], D. Roseveare et al. [OECD, 1996], W. Leibfritz et al. [OECD, 1996], OECD [1996, 1998], B. Bosworth and G. Burtless [1998], E.P. Davis [1998a,b], European Round Table [2000].

37 K. Hviding and M. Mérette [OECD, 1998].

hospital care and physicians' services, increase at a reduced rate as the age at death increases, whereas expenditures for long-term care increase at an accelerated rate. Health care spending for women is consistently higher than for men. Combined medicare and nursing home expenditures from the age of 65 years until death are 17 to 137 percent greater for women than for men, depending on the age at death. After adjustment of the increased longevity of women, cumulative costs are slightly higher for women than for men at age of death of 65 and increasing to 50 percent higher accumulated level at higher ages of death.

It has been pointed out by U.E. Reinhardt [2002] however, that the trend that health care systems will claim an ever-increasing share of resources is mainly caused by technical progress in clinical care, which affects the health care spending for all age-gender groups. On the demand side it is important to note that the income elasticity of the demand for health care in Western countries is far above 1. A higher demand for health care, thus, is a reflection of preferences of people and societies becoming more prosperous. A further cost driver on the demand side is the lack of any cost –benefit calculus and consciousness.
Concluding, not aging but other factors on both the supply side and the demand side make modern health care expensive in general.

5.2 A paradox

There appears to arise a (new) *paradox* that on a macro-level the affluent society can afford to grow older comfortably and that on a meso- and micro-level serious and prolonged budgetary and fiscal problems arise, that allegedly will impede economic development and are detrimental to the welfare of citizens. Evidently the mechanisms to levy taxes and pension plan contributions on labour income alone will produce unmanageable difficulties.
In our view budgetary and fiscal problems are not arising from the inadequacy of national resources, but they arise from the ill-shaped systems for financing public expenditures out of labour income only and not out of production. This fallacy is mainly due to accidents of history.
Not a scarcity of resources is at the basis of the affordability and sustainability of pension systems and an aging society but how and by who they are financed.

5.2.1 The method of pension finance - on a micro or personal level

Allegedly paying taxes and pension contributions out of workers' income on behalf of the elderly under a pay-as-you-go system is up from a certain point felt to be no longer or less sustainable, in the sense that it will give rise to an unacceptably high and unbearable premium level for the group of contribution payers[38]. We may add that probably such is true as well for the welfare state as a

38 Strengthening the link between contribution and benefit levels might make the (felt) burden of those contributions – e.g. an increase of 3 to 5 percentage points – easier

whole at that time as it is financed also on a pay-as-you-go basis. One may wonder under which conditions old-age social security is no longer a benefit but a burden – and when the reverse holds – as it was developed to produce more security for the elderly population?

In contrast, contribution payments under a funded scheme are less likely be regarded by individuals as taxes rather than their own savings for an old-age income provision, thereby avoiding to a large extent negative labour market distortions and probably giving rise to increased labour force participation.
Participants to a funded scheme may consider the accumulated assets as their own (collective) capital, generating returns, which from an economic point of view can be compared with labour income, but they are less visible as pension capital income usually is not paid out.
In other words, paying retirement income to the elderly out of the labour income of the workers is likely perceived as a burden. Opposed, setting aside pension capital revenues for their own retirement income purposes is viewed by individuals as being very different from paying contributions under a pay-as-you-go based pension scheme and is less likely considered as a burden, let alone as being unbearable, since the link between future benefits and current contribution payments is more clear. The returns on pension capital, in other words, contribute to a further accumulation of capital as though contributions were levied on pension capital income at a full hundred-percentage rate. As a result, budgetary and fiscal problems do not or only to a far minor extent arise.

5.2.2 The method of pension finance - on a macro or national level

It is often argued that the origins of all future pension problems, if any, is the failure to start and maintain funded pension schemes rather than pension plans pay-as-you-go financed. If public and supplementary pension plans had accumulated sufficient assets – so the argument goes – paying future pension expenditures would be less or not a problem at all.
A proviso must be made however as this 'solution' will not change the basic mechanism redistributing production among different groups of population, e.g. the retired and the non-retired. Or, in other words, basically the competition over resources raised by the pensions to be paid to the elderly is not removed by the transition from pay-as-you-go to funding. The way of pension financing does not affect in its essentials the distribution across time of the resources to be transferred to the elderly. No generation generally can store (for its own retirement purposes) the commodities that it has produced itself, apart from durable goods to some extent. Thus, for a society as a whole there can be, ceteris paribus, no redistribution of pension assets and purchasing power over time to a substantial degree. The consumptional expenditures of the elderly, today and in the future,

---

bearable and more acceptable. This can be accomplished irrespective the way of pension financing.

always has to be provided for out of current production in the same time period, irrespective of whether the pensions are funded or not[39].

Funding will be preferential to the extent that it causes the volume of national investments and national product to be higher. If certain conditions are fulfilled funding matters and could be part of the solution to the problems caused by e.g. adverse demographic developments[40]. A review of the merits and demerits of both pension finance systems, pay-as-you-go and funding is presented in Appendix C.
A further expansion of funded occupational supplementary pension plans can be considered as an adequate, but not a unique mechanism to promote savings.
Note however that pension finance systems are not created, at least not in the first place, because of the impact they might have on the performance of the national economy. Foremost, they are designed as a mechanism to adequately provide for pension incomes to the elderly.
Though the financing method may seem of minor importance as the competition over resources is not basically affected by the transferring mechanism pay-as-you or funding, pay-as-you-go opposed to funding increases labour costs in the form of higher taxes and payroll contributions, thereby giving rise to labour market distortions and threatening the competitiveness of most European countries.

5.2.3 The ownership of pension capital

Economic and social institutions like the ownership of goods and assets, embodied in pension entitlements and other social security benefits, are of much more relevance for the sustainability of old age income plans than levying taxes and contributions from labour income or capital income as there are many risks involved. Workers can evade contributions, and taxes on capital income are very difficult or not at all to enforce effectively due to the high mobility of the financial capital. Under a pay-as-you-go system benefits are more likely to be cut than contributions to be increased.
The ownership of assets comprises a claim upon physical assets and creates a claim on future production of goods and services in the economy that is generated with the joint input of labour and capital.
Pensioners are thought to be better able to fight for their share of national product as owners of capital than as lobbyists for pay-as-you-go financed pensions.
Thus, from a security point of view pensioners might prefer not to be dependent on the willingness and ability of the working population who pays the contributions to finance old-age pensions. Instead, it is preferential that the elderly possess a factor of production of their own. The ownership of (part of) the capital stock is a more secure basis for sustaining a pension scheme and minimizing its

39 The confusion, if any, originates from the tendency to generalize from the individual to the economy (*fallacy of composition*). It is a fallacy of composition to assume that because something is true for an individual it is (necessarily) true on aggregate. For instance, '... if I stand on my seat in the theatre I will get a better view, but if everybody does so, nobody will get a better view'.

40 See e.g. N. Barr [2000] and J.B. Kuné [2000].

vulnerability. It is also probable that the ownership of assets makes the process of transfer of resources less political and/or represents a safeguard against political seizure.
In a future world of immobile labour and mobile capital, it can be assumed that the long-run incidence of pension contributions is almost entirely on labour. This reinforces the relevance of the ownership of pension capital and its revenues.

No guarantees

Note, however, that guarantees cannot be given as they are in some way or other always virtual. In a pay-as-you-go scheme they are based on the strength of an implicit social contract between generations; under funding they are based on the ability of the economy always to yield an adequate return on financial assets. When, in a funded scheme, total monetary purchasing power or the demand for goods and services (largely) exceeds the value and amount of current output at prevailing prices, a general price inflation will bring them back into line. First, prices of consumer goods will rise, thereby bringing about a cut in the real income of the retired. Secondly, the elderly will see the prices of the securities they wish to sell to the younger age groups, decreasing and thereby their claims on real goods and services[41]. This means a further cut in their real purchasing power. On the other hand, under a pay-as-you-go scheme contributions will be lowered when a readjustment seems to be inevitable and consequently the real income of the pensioners will decrease proportionately. S.J. Schieber and J.B. Shoven [1997] notice there could be wide falls in asset prices. Also R. Brooks [2000] suggests that there will be an excess supply of equities in coming decades with a marked decline in the returns on retirement savings. Opposed, J.M. Poterba [1998] finds no evidence of a (strong) likelihood of a depressing effect of the demographic transition on asset prices around 2020-2030.

5.2.4 No controversy between workers and pensioners

The argument that funding and pay-as-you-go are equivalent in real economic terms has its own drawbacks as it ignores the basic nature of the economic process and of social and financial institutions in solving the distributional problem in respect of old-age.
The notion of a large volume of material goods and services being transferred from their producers – the de facto working labour population equipped with the

41 In this way e.g. P. Wallace [1999] in a popularly written, but well documented book, who is rather sceptical about many future developments. Similarly, B. Bosworth and G. Burtless [1998 (2)] are rather pessimistic about the effects of expanding domestic capital formation in the face of population aging and a falling growth rate of the labour force, involving large declines in the return of capital. Labour income will rise.
On the other hand it is observed by R. Hemming [1999] that there will not be an 'asset meltdown' as aging populations switch out of stocks. 'Asset values will adjust gradually as national and global financial markets respond in a measured way to country-specific and worldwide population aging which is well understood and quite predictable.'

national capital stock – to the elderly is artificial and not right from an economic point of view.
To consider workers and pensioners as groups with opposed interests is not correct[42]. Evidently, national product is the result of the joint input of labour and of capital and as a consequence output is divided between capital and labour – under equilibrium conditions - according to their marginal product, i.e. wage rate and profit rate. This basic distributional aspect is ignored in much of the old-age social security literature. Particularly, at least on a macro-level, the (role of the) ownership of the capital stock is frequently ignored.
The crucial issue in respect of accrued pension rights is that it constitutes a claim on future output in exchange for foregoing a part of present output. Pensioners want and need a firm and solid claim on national product in order to be able to consume the goods and services currently being produced. Under funding the retired population has at its disposal such a claim arising from their identifiable ownership of productive capital as a resource base of their own[43]. A higher labour force participation of the elderly gives also rise to such a resource base.

5.2.5 (Partial) shift from pay-as-you-go to funding

Though it cannot be shown unambiguously that funding favours national saving and economic growth, the momentum for a (partial) shift from pay-as-you-go to funding and more emphasis on capital reserve remains. Proposals for funding often primarily intend to reduce the size of intergenerational redistribution. The debate pay-as-you-go versus funding should (also) not be confused with the issue of solidarity or intra- and intergenerational redistribution.
A (partial) shift from pay-as-you-go to funding of the national basic pension plans is not without problems as there are major transitional losses involved. The generations living during the transitional period have to pay – in terms of reduced consumption – for the pensions of the preceding generations (under pay-as-you-go), while paying – in terms of savings or reduced consumption – for their own pensions under funding[44]. A conversion from pay-as-you-go to funding therefore

---

42 From a social and psychological point of view there certainly can and will be opposed interests, as future generations of retirees receive high pension incomes and are (very) wealthy as well. Cf. S.A. MacManus [1996], '... today's intergenerational differences primarily involve intensity rather than direction. [...] Tomorrow, we are more likely to find different generations supporting policy priorities that are diametrically opposed to each other as the nation undergoes its greying metamorphosis and the economic realities associated with it sink in.'

43 P.A. Diamond [1997] proposes to give social security benefit promises the same status as private contracts or private property as a means of constitutional protection and insulation against benefit reductions.

44 The present working population and the future leading edge working population presumably as well have chosen not to raise as many children as previous generations did. They can be asked therefore, it is argued, to use the expenditures saved by not raising children for financing the transitional costs of the shift from pay-as-you-go to funding rather than increasing their consumption. They are not worse off than they otherwise with an unchanged development of the population (under a pay-as-you-go system) would have

cannot be realized in a Pareto-optimal way without extra costs involved for at least one generation (F. Breyer, 1990). Thus, once a pay-as-you-go system has been introduced, it is often argued, practically speaking all generations are captured or 'locked-in', even when the funding system would generate the necessary savings for sustained economic growth. If a pension reform succeeds in reducing distortions prevailing in the economy and in ameliorating the functioning of factor markets and political and institutional processes, a Pareto-improvement is possible[45]. If the gains from reducing those distortions are sufficiently large, public debt policy may be useful in facilitating the shift towards more funding in pension finance.

In addition, the transition burden should not be dramatized. In the case of Germany it is shown by A. Börsch-Supan [1998] that the transition burden is about 4 percent of average household income, relatively moderate and far from a 'double burden'. In the second place workers in turn obtain property rights of capital goods – yielding investment revenues – for reduced consumption. Furthermore, the working of factor markets in many countries can be ameliorated, leading to shifts in the allocation of labour and capital which induce higher efficiency and gain in welfare despite the transition burden[46]. The question arises whether the efficiency gains are important enough to finance the transition and to compensate, at least in part, without too many distortions those who will lose during the transition period.
The functioning of the labour market can be improved as distortions in the labour supply are removed. As a result labour supply increases, which in turn reduces the wage level and heightens the return on the domestic capital stock. This makes possible a Pareto-efficient transition to a funded system[47]. A large potential for Pareto-improvement can also be achieved when pension institutions invest in higher yielding assets than government debt, whereas the legislated pay-as-you-go based pension promises are transformed in public debt that earn the market rate of

---

been. After the transition future generations under funding pay pension contributions that, ceteris paribus, mainly depend on the real rate of return on capital and not on the number of children they have. Though less future labour supply will increase the wage rate and lower capital returns.
See for the transition from pay-as-you-go to funding e.g. various contributions in H. Siebert [1998] and R. Disney [2000].

45 B.U. Wigger [2002] demonstrates the possibility of a Pareto-improving public (pay-as-you-go based) pension reform. Such reform consists of implementing a transfer scheme that links individual public pension benefits to individual young-age human capital investment. Thereby the public pension program provide an efficient signal of the social benefits of human capital formation.

46 A. Börsch-Supan, Ludwig, A. and J.K. Winter [2002]. On the other hand, the transition costs can increase considerably by high administration costs often associated with funded schemes, especially systems based on individual accounts (though less so in a compulsory scheme) plus insurance costs for mitigating the volatility, if a DC-scheme is used.

47 See e.g. D.P. Broer and E.W.M.T. Westerhout [1996]. Note, however, that as a principle, no Pareto-improving transition is possible if individual pension benefits are proportional to individual contributions, which happens to be the case in e.g. Germany, but not in the Netherlands (cf. R. Fenge [1995]).

return[48]. Nonetheless, there are no simple solutions. Dismantling the welfare state or advocating doing nothing (no reform measures) are not viable options.

Concluding

We find ourselves in a Pareto-efficient world that nonetheless yields a lower rate of return on contributions (under pay-as-you-go) than a funded system for all generations except the first. We may wish therefore to make a break-through considering states of the world that originate from alternative economic, government debt and pension policies generating more gains for all future generations and a loss for one current generation only.

In the (most fully) funded strategy all pension payments and the further accumulation of pension capital are financed from the returns on capital, opposed to a full pay-as-you-go based system in which all pension payments are financed by the current working population.

It can be necessary to resist political majorities that insist on maintaining pay-as-you-go based systems, though funding is preferential in the long term. It is likely that at the same time there will be some need for reducing of the pension provisions during the transitional period and maybe even of those nearing retirement today.

5.2.6 Pitfalls: the public versus private issue

Generally funded schemes are identified as being private and pay-as-you-go schemes as public. A preference for funding as an adequate instrument to cope with the aging problem can easily be transformed into a more general preference for private pensions and being part of a wider argument for privatisation and less interference of politics and government with pension providers in a commercial market. L.H. Thompson [1995, p. 67]: '... people with less taste for redistribution will be more likely to favour private-sector approaches, and those who favour private-sector approaches may do so, precisely because they prefer less distribution.'

Note however that public schemes are not necessarily restrained to pay-as-you-go and, conversely, funded based pension plans are not necessarily privately managed. Hence, the public versus private issue should not be confused with the debate pay-as-you-go versus funding. The objective to increase national saving by a higher degree of funding in pension finance can be achieved with either publicly or privately managed pension funds.

Proposals for funding often primarily intend to reduce the size of intergenerational redistribution.

The debate pay-as-you-go versus funding should (also) not be confused either with the issue of solidarity or intra- and intergenerational redistribution or with the issue of the defined benefit versus defined contribution form of the pension formula. Defined contribution schemes contain redistribute elements if pension savings are invested on a collective basis rather than individually.

---

48 Cf. S. Valdés-Prieto [1997].

5.3 Concluding observations

It can be argued that the aging of societies will lead to less innovation, disserving and disinvestments. Productivity and technical progress also come to a halt. Or, in other words, the problems might be worse than projected in many studies. There is natural tendency of pessimists to depict apocalyptically almost the end of civilization and it is natural tendency of optimists to want to believe that the problems are not that bad. The pessimistic outcomes may, in fact, not occur. There is slight probability that some danger (or in part) comes through and if that happens, their impact would be dramatically severe. Therefore adequate policy measures on a broad scale in all countries should be taken to make sure that the chances of bad outcomes are greatly reduced.
It has been made clear in chapter 4. before that pensioners throughout time as a rule are better off than their parents at those same ages and in our analyses they (deliberately) also fare well relative to the working age population at that time.
It is a preconceived idea that each retired generation should have a standard of living comparable to that of current workers rather than comparable to their own standard of living when young or middle-aged. The question arises, however, whether the issue of indexation is actually important for policy purposes? Particularly, to the extent that the welfare of the retirees results from their own choices (viz. voluntary early retirement and preference for leisure), their situation is of less direct policy concern, probably not at all.

The increase in the labour force participation rate and an adequate annual productivity growth necessary to compensate for the adverse effects of aging and to enable a further rise in welfare do not take place automatically. Instead, they pose huge challenges to economic and social institutions.
Most national and international studies on aging tend to focus on social policy issues (pensions, health care). As pointed out, population aging is more; it will change the macro-economic balance in many countries, primarily through factor prices. Though this is not a new insight for experts, the policy debate tends to get lost by one-sided interest in the sustainability of pension and health care schemes and the need for pension reform and fiscal policy measures. Availability of labour and capital and their respective rates of return are at least of equal importance, if not more.

Policy guidelines defined at the EU-level and individual member states often disappoint by their failure to present a clear and comprehensive strategy for dealing with the process of population aging, as they heavily focus on the fiscal and budgetary implications of pension reform measures. Though understandable, this happens to the neglect of generating the national product and its growth rate, let alone the income distributional consequences over time of policy actions, which, at least in the long run, are crucial for the political and generational sustainability of all reform processes. Economic growth should remain the central policy objective, while at the same time budgetary sustainability is not ignored.
Policies to be pursued in the face of aging are dealt with in the next chapter.

6 Policies in the face of aging

It has been shown conclusively before that we in the more developed societies can afford to grow older rather comfortably. In most more developed countries pensions predominantly are paid out of part of workers' income under a pay-as-you go financing system. In as far as the labour force declines and productivity slows down, it makes sense to be concerned about workers' capacity to pay the taxes and contributions necessary to match the pension and health care obligations. In less developed countries generally intra-family support systems prevail; there is no comparable aging problem.

6.1 Introductory observations

Preventing a decline in labour supply can be realized from increased labour force participation by those of working age (reducing unemployment) and importing labour (either directly by selective immigration or indirectly by exporting capital abroad) and, most powerful, raising the age of retirement[49]. Increasing labour force participation will also diminish the amount of (means-tested) social assistance expenditures.

Increased output per worker can arise from increases in the quantity (and quality) of the capital stock the working force is equipped with, and from growth in the quality of labour.

Hence, the policy strategy first centres on achieving an increase in the average number of years people spend active in the labour force. Concurrently, policies that aim at augmenting productivity will help support improvements in living standards. Secondly, to avoid severe fiscal imbalances, substantial increases in public debt and/or unacceptable rises in contribution rates policy measures should be directed at creating sources other than pay-as-you-go based public pension payments in providing retirement income. As observed, there are no simple solutions, let alone fully satisfactory. Policy actions are required at many fronts. Part of its framework is exposed in the following sections.

Furthermore, useful and necessary – and at the basis of policies to promote participation and productivity – is a broad range of policies in respect of sound macroeconomic management, openness to international trade and competition, a tax system that encourages work effort and entrepreneurship, and government expenditures programs directed to investments and capital accumulation.

Budgetary reform measures aim at removing fiscal imbalances and reducing public debt, thereby diminishing the amount of interest payments on debt, which allegedly is beneficial for the economy. Appropriate regulations in financial markets and product and factor markets are also of relevance in stimulating innovation and

---

49 Note that increasing welfare may (on a micro-level) stimulate people to retire earlier, frustrating the (macro) policy goal to increase the average age of retirement.

productivity growth. Above all, governments need the flexibility and courage to reallocate categories of public expenditures. The main challenge for public policy in the face of aging therefore is not only how to deal with trends towards higher public spending, but also how to deal with necessary institutional, political and administrative reallocations.

6.2 Policy measures to enlarge the contribution or resource base

Policy measures to broaden the contribution base by increasing the size and quality of the labour force therefore should aim at (1) stimulating investments in the human capital of the working age population and its labour force participation as well, (2) encouraging investments in physical capital domestically or abroad, in infrastructure and in R&D programs[50].

Investments in labour supply and human capital include,

- policies to reduce public debt (leading to less interest payments, thereby alleviating government budgets) and to restrain increased taxes (necessary to finance public pensions and public health care) in order to reduce distortionary effects;
- policies to raise the labour force participation by reducing official unemployment, eliminating the poverty trap and above all, other forms of non-employment by adequate labour market regulatory reforms[51];
- particularly for some countries policies to increase the female labour force participation rate by e.g. creating child-care facilities and reducing the tax-wedge on labour income;
- policies to increase the labour force participation of the older workers[52] by,
  - reducing moral hazard in social security schemes (early withdrawal, disability and unemployment schemes) and eliminating the disincentives and other penalties for older workers to remain active in the labour force;
  - making pension schemes (and other social security measures) more actuarially fair on an individual level[53] and removing fiscal disincentives for

---

50 See also OECD [1996, 1998, 2000b], Group of Ten [1998], D. Turner et al. [1998].

51 As soon as (near) full employment is attained, new problems will arise. That is of labour mobility. In a situation of labour shortages for certain skills in certain regions, the need for enhanced mobility of labour within the EU-15 and migration (also from outside the EU-15) will grow.

52 Unused labour capacity between the ages 55 and 65 ranges from 67 percent for Belgium to 35 percent for Sweden (it is 37 percent in the US and 22 percent in Japan).

53 S.Blöndal and S. Scarpetta [OECD, 1999] estimated that achieving actuarial neutrality in pension schemes in many developed countries would have the effect of raising labour force participation rates of males aged 55-65 by about 3 to 4 percentage points, representing a return approximating the situation prevailing in the early 1979's. In countries where the financial incentives for early retirement were particularly large (Finland, France, Italy, the

delayed retirement and eliminating over-generous or all incentives for early retirement[54], access to disability, unemployment and social welfare schemes, increasing the age of entitlement to full pension, increasing the length of the contribution period for full benefit and above all, decreasing the size of the informal or shadow economy and;
    - bringing into line wage rate and productivity, leading to lower earnings for older workers and improving job opportunities;
- policies to increase productivity by further training, retraining and education of the present workforce, stimulating R&D programs and up to a certain extent increasing the capital-output ratio in production (capital deepening). As the decrease in the relative size of the economically active population can only partly be offset by a higher (physical) capital intensity (in turn limited by diminishing returns), growth in labour productivity predominantly has to be provided for by strengthening the education, skills and abilities of the working age population (human capital);
- policies to increase productivity of the future labour force by (more and better) education of those now younger than 20 years of age and stimulating parents to invest widely in the human capital of their children[55]. Facilities for child-care and other allowances must make possible combined high female labour force participation, fertility at replacement level and accumulation of human capital particularly in young children.

6.2.1 Shifting factor scarcity

Capital supply is expected to be relatively abundant in the coming decades. This is another way of saying that the rate of return on capital is likely to decline. However, if private savings fall short of what is necessary for sustained growth (leading to an increase in the interest rate), there is not much a government can do to mobilize new savings, except from running a budgetary surplus thereby creating a source of saving of its own[56].

Netherlands, Portugal), the participation rate of older workers can increase by about 8 to 9 percentage points.

54 Many countries have brought about increases in the retirement age. Germany is increasing the minimal pensionable age from 63 to 65 years for males (over the period 2001 - 2009) and from 60 to 65 for females (over the years 2011 - 2018). Italy (with currently one of the lowest retirement ages, at 50 for females and 55 for males) will increase retirement age for both sexes to 60 by 2001 and thereafter up to 65. In the UK the retirement age for females will be increased and be brought into line with that of males from 60 to 65, starting with those to retire in 2010 and completing the process in 2020. In the US an unreduced pension is payable at an age of 67 by 2022 and it is proposed to raise that age to 70. In Japan the age of retirement is increased from 60 to 65 by 2014 for males and by 2019 for females.

55 Cf. L.A. Bovenberg [2002].

56 Turner et al. [1998] found that combined adequate reform measures could have a significant impact on levels of welfare. In Europe living standards can rise by 2½ percent a year in the coming decades, a growth rate higher than any time since the 1970's. Similarly K. McMorrow and W. Roeger [1999]: the effect of combining all reform measures – keeping public budgets close to zero, pension reforms, raising labour force participation rates by

Increasing scarcity of labour relative to physical capital and the resulting higher wage level relative to capital returns will provide strong incentives for investment in human capital, which combined with higher labour force participation, can more than compensate for the adverse effects of population aging on the economy. Technological progress to a large degree embodied in human capital is generally considered as a major factor of economic growth in the context of a knowledge-based economy.

Note that scarcity of labour may also give rise to labour saving technological change and wage increase will then be less pronounced.

Naturally, human capital is embodied in people with finite lifetimes. The returns of human capital investments are the discounted sum of future wages. Therefore, the higher future wages are, the more favourable it is – more favourable than investing in physical capital – for young people to invest in their education and training but also for middle-aged workers if they decide to remain longer in the labour force. Higher wage levels may also stimulate labour force participation, particularly of those now not employed, viz. women and people over 55 years of age.

Concluding

The growth rate of human capital may more than offset the decreasing or even negative growth rate of population and its detrimental effect on the economy. However, this is not an automatic process. We are not sure that greater returns on investment in human capital will provoke more investments of people in their education and skills and we are not sure that higher wages stimulate labour force participation. Thus, there may be need for adequate policy measures to encourage people to invest in their human capital if they do not have sufficient stimulus to make those investments themselves.

6.2.2 Provisos

In Europe most public schemes – including disability, unemployment and early retirement schemes – are rather generous for early retirement and tend to punish later retirement. In addition, new technologies make the skills of older workers obsolete and those workers may choose or are pressed, particularly in countries with high unemployment levels, to leave the labour force.

Removing disincentives to work after the early retirement age is highly recommended and will do a great deal to actually increase the participation rate of the 55-64 olds[57].

Labour force participation trends are not fixed forever. Changing incentives at least in part change behaviour. Later retirement is the more efficient as it not only reduces the number of pensioners, but also increases the number of active persons

about 10 percentage points and regulatory changes to boost productivity – is that Europe can entirely overcome the impact of aging.

57 OECD Working Paper 202, 'The retirement decision in OECD countries': removing disincentive to work could increase the participation by 4 to 8 percentage points.

available to pay taxes and contributions. Note however that in practical terms people cannot be forced to stay in the labour force, as the demand for leisure is a reflection of preferences of people and societies becoming more prosperous. People nowadays desire and expect to retire at relatively young ages. There is not much a government can do to change the preferences of people for earlier retirement, using their due to income increase ever larger saving accounts – even when fiscal incentives for pension saving are removed – and hence from that time on to consume more than they produce. This is rather fundamental. Moreover, the coice of leisure and working time should not be distorted by government policies as it reduces optimality.

It is hardly realistic to think that the effective retirement age can be increased rather easily by five years or more[58]. In contrast, it will appear difficult to stop the trend towards earlier withdrawal from the labour force. Many people decide to retire earlier rather than later if it is financially feasible. Changing the behaviour of people is significantly more strenuous than to change rules.

Hence, to begin with, fiscal incentives for pension saving aimed at earlier retirement, must be eliminated as soon as possible. Such policy measures, necessary as they are, are likely to induce intergenerational conflict and debate. Huge tensions will arise between fiscal government policy and the preferences of people approaching retirement age. One could go one step further by imposing a grey-, leisure or retirement tax (unless seriously disabled) thereby discouraging (early) retirement and stimulating staying in the labour force.

An increase in retirement age might also induce lower saving rates. Retiring at older ages raises lifetime income and pension benefits in the retirement phase. As a result private savings would decline, resulting in lower growth[59]. Allowing for increased longevity, on the other hand can stimulate saving.

6.3 The impact of reform policy measures

The OECD is rather optimistic about the effects of a comprehensive policy package to address the adverse impact of aging[60]. Policies that succeed in reducing the rate of structural unemployment to levels recorded in the late 1960's, policies that raise the labour force participation – that of older males by 7 to 9 percentage points or more in countries with particularly large distortions in their pension systems, e.g. France, Italy and the Netherlands, by 4 to 6 percentage points in most other

58 P.M. Liedtke (secretary-general of the Geneva Association, [2001]) highly recommends the broad introduction of part-time work arrangements for people who would otherwise retire completely. Liedtke is very optimistic about the capacities of older workers, they are experienced, reliable, work hard, are effective in their job, think before they act and display good team-working abilities. In contrast, one could imagine that an older workforce is less conducive to innovation and technological change, less entrepreneurial and ambitious and therefore less productive.

59 K. Futagami and T. Nakajima [2001].

60 D. Turner et al. [1998] and OECD, *Reforms for an ageing society*, Paris, 2000a.

European countries and by less than 4 percent in North America and Japan[61] - and policies that raise the labour force participation of women towards 'best practice' levels achieved in Scandinavian countries, will raise output growth by an extra 0.75 percentage point per annum in Europe, 0.5 percentage point in Japan and a modest 0.25 percentage point in the US. Hence, a combined package of reform measures is estimated to raise output levels by over 40 percent in the EU-15, 30 percent in Japan and 15 percent in the US by 2050. In the case of Europe, the right combination of reform options can even lead to higher growth rates than the region has experienced in the past.
Real interest rates in the EU-15 countries could fall by about 1.5 point in the first half-century relative to the reference scenario from close to 5 percent in 2000 to 3.5 percent in 2050. Similar declines in the real interest rate occur in the US and Japan.

An aging study of the European Commission (DG Economic and Financial Affairs; K. McMorrow and W. Roeger [1999]) arrives at similar results as found in the OECD reports. Without any offsetting policy adjustments annual per capita growth of GDP would be 0.5 percent less relative to the baseline scenario, where the adverse effects of aging on the labour market and public expenditures are disregarded. In the comprehensive reform scenario the increase of GDP not only compensates for the detrimental effects of aging but GDP can grow by an extra annual 0.1 percent relative to the baseline scenario. Thus, if the right combination of reforms is chosen the EU-15 can entirely overcome the impact of aging and increase the level of GDP by an additional 5 percent in 2050.
In a follow-up study late 2001 similar findings were published. More details are given in Appendix F[62].

6.3.1 Feedback mechanisms

Otherwise, it should be observed that even when no policy measures are taken some economic mechanisms would start to work. There are allegedly numerous institutional and market feedback mechanisms in modern economies that guarantee that most of the adverse consequences of population aging predicted are offset to a substantial degree. Aging will make labour more scarce and this will lead to lower unemployment and, through the mechanism of higher wages, will lead to higher participation rates and will also create incentives for investment in human capital. In a forward looking, rational expectations framework young people may anticipate

---

61 The case of Switzerland with a labour force participation rate of 82 percent for men of 55 to 65 years of age demonstrates conclusively that early retirement is by no means inevitable.

62 In the 2001-study the baseline scenario is defined as the scenario with population projections based on Eurostat and participation rates at their 2000 level, no further reduction in the effective retirement age and also the generosity of the pension system (net retirement rate) assuming at its 2000 level. The late 1999 study of K. McMorrow and W. Roeger assumes broad adherence to the EU's *Stability and Growth Pact* where deficits at the central government level are disappeared by 2003 an the debt to GDP ratio is expected to be around 60 percent in 2003 and to stay at that level through 2050. Population is furthermore still growing at the rate witnessed during the last decades of the 20th century.

that their pension benefits will be eroded by adverse demographic developments and increase their private savings. Nonetheless the question remains whether market economies may or may not be able to create sufficient adaptive mechanisms to respond to changing patterns of scarcity of labour and capital.

6.3.2 Required labour force participation to maintain welfare

In Table 6 are shown the participation ratios necessary to maintain per capita welfare by 2020 and 2050 on its year 2000 level in the more developed countries (Table 6A) and in the transitional economies and less developed countries (Table 6B). The reader will find interesting evidence.
The average participation rate in EU-15 in 2000 is estimated at about 0.68, which can roughly be divided in a female activity rate of 0.51 and a male activity rate of 0.85.
A moderate increase of the effective retirement age and retaining the present growth in the female labour force participation are leading to a participation rate of 0.73 in 2020 (the female rate then being 0.59 and the male rate 0.87), which is necessary and sufficient to maintain welfare at its original level in 2000[63].

A 10 percentage point increase in the EU-15's labour force participation from 0.68 in 2000 to 0.78 in 2050 is quite well possible to achieve, bringing the EU-level back up at the US-level in 2000. The required participation rate for retaining constant welfare levels – assuming zero productivity growth – in the EU-15 by 2050 is still much higher, 0.85 on average and 0.89 in the US. Such a high levels of participation are considered not to be attainable.
In Japan the required participation exceeds even 100 percent. The transitional economies are similar to the EU-15 countries; the Czech Republic stands out with 107 percent.
In most developing countries the required ratio in 2050 to maintain welfare at its 2000-level is not much higher than in 2020, reflecting the demographic dividend that can be reaped.

Concluding

We may conclude that the better countries succeed to implement widespread labour market reforms, resulting in lower unemployment and higher labour force participation rates, the less they will experience adverse effects from an aging population. As demonstrated in paragraph 4.3.5 productivity growth to maintain (and increase) welfare is the most powerful instrument.

---

63 Cf. European Commission [2001]: ' ... bringing back the effective retirement age, which is close to 60 today in the EU-15, to 65 gradually over the next ten years, has a significant effect on the level of GDP, with the latter growing by over 13 percent in 2050 compared with the baseline scenario, thereby going a long way towards offsetting the GDP loss associated with ageing.'

Table 6A. Participation ratio necessary to maintain per capita welfare in 2020 and 2050 on its 2000-level (EU-15, US, Canada and Japan; zero productivity growth)

	Participation ratio		
Country	2000 (actual)	2020	2050
(1)	(2)	(3)	(4)
EU-15	**0.68**	**0.73**	**0.85**
Belgium	0.64	0.67	0.76
France	0.68	0.72	0.79
Germany	0.71	0.76	0.87
Italy	0.60	0.64	0.80
Netherlands	0.71	0.77	0.85
Spain	0.64	0.67	0.88
Sweden	0.76	0.81	0.87
UK	0.76	0.79	0.88
Other world			
US	0.78	0.83	0.89
Canada	0.77	0.82	0.91
Japan	0.78	0.92	1.04

Table 6B. **Participation ratio necessary to maintain per capita welfare on its 2000-level (Eastern Europe and less developed countries; zero productivity growth)**

	Participation ratio		
Country	2000 (actual)	2020	2050
(1)	(2)	(3)	(4)
Eastern Europe			
Russia	0.70	0.72	0.82
Ukraine	0.70	0.71	0.81
Poland	0.69	0.71	0.85
Czech Republic	0.80	0.86	1.07
Romania	0.70	0.71	0.86
Hungary	0.60	0.63	0.75
Other world			
China	0.70	0.70	0.81
India	0.70	0.66	0.69
Pakistan	0.70	0.60	0.60
Indonesia	0.70	0.68	0.73
Iran	0.70	0.60	0.67
Turkey	0.70	0.66	0.76
Brazil	0.70	0.67	0.76
Mexico	0.70	0.69	0.73
Argentina	0.70	0.69	0.73
Egypt	0.70	0.64	0.68
Nigeria	0.70	0.59	0.67
Kenya	0.70	0.58	0.57
South Africa	0.70	0.69	0.67

6.3.3 Policy measures in respect of pensions

It seems likely that pay-as-you-go based public pension systems, because of rising budgetary pressures and the need to balance pension payments and contributions, at least in relative terms will show some future cuts in their generosity, leading to lower pension levels which will encourage people to retire later and work longer.
Policy measures to lessen the increase in contribution rates, thereby avoiding high labour costs, therefore should aim at creating a resource base not only independent on the labour earning capacity of the retirees themselves, but independent on the earning capacity of the labour force and of other tax payers as well. This can be realized by funding as a method of pension finance. This issue was discussed before in chapter 5.

Furthermore, pension saving can increase total national saving when certain conditions are fulfilled.
A higher level of savings makes possible a higher level of investments and a larger physical capital stock, leading to a larger future resource base and a larger future national product. Pension savings are a large part of total private savings in e.g. the UK, Ireland and the Netherlands. To increase pension savings, apart from fiscal privileges and stimuli, more emphasis should be laid on the (funded) supplementary pension system, hence a new balance between collective and individual responsibilities[64].
Finally we want to emphasize that pension schemes, whether they are public or private, should not contain automatisms, particularly in respect of indexing accrued pension rights. Undesired solidarities in pension plans must be removed by establishing more actuarial fairness on an individual level.

The debate of old age and population aging has to move beyond pension scheme preoccupation. Instead, its focus is on broadening the resource base of the society as a whole and ensuring that pension scheme designs are not a barrier to this. While financial incentives to early retirement in most EU-15 countries are gradually removed, the adverse attitudes to older workers have not been captured. The role of the fourth pillar is badly understood.

National policy measures should be complemented by relevant measures at the EU-level in two ways, a) measures to coordinate national macroeconomic, employment and pension reform policies and b) measures to complete the internal market in financial services and labour (removing barriers to cross-border mobility of labour).

---

64 To the extent that a linkage exists between contributions paid and acquired pension rights, paying contributions will be preferred to general taxes. This linkage can be established by an actuarially fair funded system, but also by a notional system where such a linkage exists without funding.

Reviews

An outline of old-age social security programs throughout the world is presented by ILO [2000]. A review of the main characteristics of the pension systems and recent reform measures taken in seventeen industrial countries is given by OECD [2000^{a}]. Furthermore, to mention a few, G. Hughes & J. Stewart [2000], K.-J. Gern [2001], JETRO [2001] and R. Disney & P. Johnson [2001]. A concise survey of the pension system and recent reform measures for eleven EU-15 countries – Denmark, Finland, Greece and Luxemburg are not included – is presented by M. Tinker et al. [2002]. Ten European country studies – including Finland and the Eastern European countries Poland, Hungary and Romania – are found in M. Feldstein & H. Siebert [2002].

6.3.4 Different views of the European Commission

Different views on how to reform old-age social security systems exist in Europe. Preference for a multi-pillar system and more emphasis on funding in financing pensions is expressed by the Economic and Financial Affairs Council and the Economic Policy Committee [2000, 2001].

It is argued that behind the social security system of every EU-15 member state a distict history lies. It is the result of a political negotiation and decision-making process. In the words of F. Vandenbroucke, '... each member state actually embodies a welfare state *sui generis*, and nearly every member state wants to keep it this way. Thus, the social welfare functions that inform the governments' policies may be very different. Still the national welfare states face highly similar challenges.'[65] As a consequence, the national public systems don't need to be transformed to funded based supplementary schemes to a large extent.

The Employment and Social Affairs Council and the Social Protection Committee recommend the so-called open method of coordination as a learning tool in reforming the social security system. Open coordination – first mentioned at the Lisbon Summit in March 2000 – is a process where explicit, clear and mutually agreed common objectives are defined, after which peer review enables member states to examine and learn from best practices in Europe. Every member state has to present every year an action plan to achieve the given objectives and these national action plans are reviewed by the European Commission and the other member states.

If the sustainability of the public pension system is endangered as other essental government expenditures are crowded out or if it is only sustainable on the basis of unacceptably high taxes and contributions, the so-called Musgrave's fixed relative income position (of pensioners and the working age population) is proposed as a solution. Demographic and economic risks are divided intergenerational fairly between both parties: rising contributions are accompanied by lower pension incomes. Creating a situation that is unsustainable in the long run is highly unfair to the generations to come.

65 F. Vandenbroucke [2001, 2002], G. Esping-Andersen et al. [2001].

6.3.5 Choosing a pension plan, the 'third road'

Defined benefit (final pay) plans are considered as too expensive and, above all, as too risky for the participants as a group; defined contribution plans are considered as too risky for individual participants with a private pension account.
A hybrid pension plan based on 'pension points' – denoted as the third road – is presented below and can be recommended as it combines the best features of both defined benefit plans and defined contribution plans. Several distinctive features of this pension-points-plan stand out. First, benefits of workers and pensioners accrue as under a defined contribution plan (average pay type), but benefits do not directly vary with investment results as up to certain extent a surplus can be used and contributions can be raised to stabilize benefit levels. Secondly, as the pension scheme proposed is mandatory, a flat rate premium system or rising with age to some degree is used. Thirdly, pension assets are managed and invested on a pooled basis rather than in individual accounts, giving rise to higher investment revenues. Investment preferences of individuals and pension institutions differ as they are related to their respective time horizons. The older the worker, the shorter the time horizon. For an institution which is an ongoing entity, on the other hand, the time horizon might be almost infinite. Fourth, the hybrid system allows for flexible portability of accrued pension rights.

Given the accrual rate, every 1000 Euro worker's income yields one pension point. Hence, the number of pension points acquired in year [t,t+1),

$$Pension\ points_t = Income_t / 1000 \qquad (1)$$

Accrued pension rights of a worker at time t, contingent upon the number of pension points, the accrual rate, the length of past working time (α) and the indexation rate applicable to past service time, amount to,

$$Accrued\ pension\ rights_t = \sum_{\tau=t-\alpha}^{t} Pension\ points_\tau * (1000 * accrual\ rate) * \prod_{\tau'=t-\alpha}^{t} (1 + indexation\ rate\_past\ service_{\tau'}) \qquad (2)$$

After retirement (at time t) benefits in year [t+γ, t+γ+1) accrue according to the indexation rate applicable to pensioners,

$$Pension\ benefit_{t+\gamma} = Pension\ benefit_t * \prod_{\delta=1}^{\gamma}(1 + indexation\ rate\_pensioners_{t+\delta}) \qquad (3)$$

6.3.6 Immigration

It has been argued that higher immigration could improve the old-age dependency ratio (the ratio of people over 65 years of age to the number of people of ages between 20 and 64). The United Nations Population Division [2000] conclude that '... among the demographic variables only international migration could be instrumental in addressing population decline and population aging in the short to medium term.' A fortiori it is advantageous to attract highly equipped and skilled foreign workers as a partial response to skilled labour shortages. It appears to be difficult, if not impossible, however to control the composition of immigration. Note also that immigration of skilled workers into the host country means that the source country will lose its most qualified workers (the well-known brain drain) and as a result its economic development will suffer.

The level of immigration to prevent a population decline in e.g. Germany would be 17.2 million over the next 50 years; Germany's current population being 82.8 million. To prevent a decline in the working force it would take 24.3 million and to keep the old-age dependency ratio constant, it would require 182 million in the half century or 3.6 million per year. Still higher immigration numbers in relative terms arise for Japan and Italy. Integration of the present part of 10 percent of immigrants has appeared already an immense task.

Even for the US the number of immigrants to keep the old-age dependency ratio constant is fairly high, 595 million over the next 50 years or 11.9 million a year. The actual forecasts for the US are 38 million or 0.76 million a year, three times the number of immigrants needed to keep the US population constant. Immigration often includes complete families and, thus, does hardly change the balance between generations.

Hence, immigration cannot play a major role in addressing the challenging of an aging population. Apart from psychological and political resistance of large numbers of immigrants, research in the Netherlands has shown conclusively that the costs of immigration in the second half of the 20th century greatly exceeded the benefits[66]. In many European countries large-scale, uncontrolled immigration of low qualified people has actually aggravated the problems by posing large additional burdens on their welfare states rather than helping to alleviate them. Immigration of unskilled labour therefore is strongly dissuaded.

---

66 Cf. N. van Nimwegen and G. Beets [2000]. W. Franssen [2002]: '...in the Netherlands there is an ever growing consensus that a large influx of workers from outside the EU cannot provide a long-term solution for the Netherlands, especially considering the huge scale on which this would have to take place. This is a view that has also been adopted by the Dutch government. The main considerations are the following: 1) migrant workers are on average followed by four family members, 2) integration of immigrants is an extremely difficult process, 3) the level of education and skills do not match the needs of the Dutch labour market, leading to much higher unemployment amongst allochthones than amongst autochthones, 4) immigation has led to a heavier burden on the social secuirty system rather than to the intended broadening of its financial basis.

6.3.7 Required immigration to maintain welfare

Table 7 shows that the labour force in the EU-15 by 2020 must be 12.2 percent larger to ensure a constant per capita welfare level, assuming zero productivity growth and unchanged labour force participation. The 12.2 percent increase in employment is realized by immigration from outside the EU-15. Rather small differences exist between EU-15 member states in 2020.
By 2050 the labour force in the EU-15 must be a huge 43.6 percent larger to retain welfare at its original level of 2000, broadly varying between one third (Belgium, France, the UK and Sweden) and two thirds (Italy and Spain) of the size of the original labour force. The Netherlands and Germany take on an intermediate position.

However, there is also the crucial question, as raised by A.L. Hillman [2002], whether immigration will be consistent with the continuation of the social contract of intergenerational transfers. Solving the demographic aging by immigation presumes that the institutions and norms that underlie the transfer system will be sustained, particularly by the willingness to pay taxes and contributions. In countries where immigrants come from – in their societies the family, tribe or clan is the primary form of social security – , the social custom may be not to pay taxes and to distrust any government. And the government happens to be the intermediator of intergenerational transfers in Western countries. The immigrants may wish not to ascribe to the continuation of the intergenerational contract. In that case, the immigration that was intended to rescue the system of intergenerational tranfers can bring the system to an end.

Concluding

There are no simple solutions. Clearly we have to solve the problems of aging ourselves by increasing the labour force participation and, above all, increasing productivity by strengthening the abilities and qualities of the (working age) population. Further welfare growth actually can only be realized by increasing productivity of the present work force. Hence, productivity growth should remain the central economic policy objective, though not to the neglect of fiscal sustainability.

6.3.8 Investing abroad

In general terms, differences of the demographic transition across countries and regions will induce international capital flows[67]. Therefore, we now turn to the possibilities of using assets abroad – particularly publicly owned foreign currency and foreign currency owned by pension funds, insurance companies and individual citizens – to alleviate the burden of the retirement income system. In principle, a society can be a net lender on the international capital markets during the working

67 This mechanism is already at work. Private net capital flows (making up about 80 percent of total world capital flows) have increased remarkably during the 1990's (M. Higgins [1999].

Table 7. Number of immigrants necessary (as a percentage of the working age population at that point of time) to maintain per capita welfare in 2020 and 2050 on its 2000-level (EU-15, US, Canada and Japan; zero productivity growth, unchanged participation rate)

Country	Immigration	
	2020	2050
(1)	(2)	(3)
EU-15	**12.2**	**43.6**
Belgium	10.4	33.0
France	11.3	30.6
Germany	15.1	44.6
Italy	13.0	60.1
Netherlands	16.9	41.0
Spain	8.9	68.7
Sweden	13.5	30.0
UK	8.8	32.8
Other world		
US	13.0	29.6
Canada	13.4	39.1
Japan	38.6	73.4

period of the baby boom cohorts and liquidate its foreign investments during those cohorts' retirement years. Or, in present circumstances a society can run a current account surplus now and a current account deficit during its aging period[68]. Total income available in future years will be increased.
A policy of higher savings and investment as observed can be helpful in offsetting some of the future burden of population aging. The extra savings can be invested in the public or private sector[69], domestically or abroad. The distributional consequences of the latter two alternatives differ. Investing in the domestic sector drives down rates of return on capital due to a higher capital intensity. On the other hand wage rates will rise as a result of higher labour productivity. Furthermore, labour supply may be too small to absorb the larger capital stock. If all or most of the extra savings flow abroad, the domestic rate of return on capital will not decline as much, but the domestic labour force will not receive then the productivity gains that they otherwise would have had. Instead, foreign workers will enjoy higher wages as a result of a capital deepening of their economies.
Furthermore, funding opens a global dimension of diversifying risks by the globalisation of capital markets, which is unavailable in a pay-as-you-go system[70].

---

68 Increased investment abroad may alleviate the aging problem in the 'western' developed countries. Note however that virtually all the major (and smaller) developed countries will have the same problem in nearly the same time period ahead. The aging 'western' world as a whole has only a rather small foreign sector. Or, in other words, not all societies can play the same game at the same time. Japan, for instance, has during the last few decades invested its current account surpluses abroad, to a large extent however in countries which also face an aging problem. Realising overseas assets Japan – on a macro-level – may probably solve at least in part its aging problem but at the expense of making the problem of those other countries worse. Remember the world as 'one global village'.

69 Opposed to often-heard arguments it is of less relevance for the performance of the economy whether the (public) pension capital is invested in public or private (corporate) assets. If a public pension fund invests in government bonds, then from the point of view of the consolidated collective sector (government and social security institutions together) funding and pay-as-you-go are similar, so the argument goes, as future interest payments to the fund have to be financed from general tax revenues.
Note however that, if the pension fund purchased government debt, a larger proportion of households' savings can be used to finance investments in the private sector. And otherwise, if the pension funds' savings were instead invested in private debt and equities, a larger part of households' savings can be used to meet public demand for capital. Or, in other words, in both cases higher savings associated with pension funding will lead to a higher demand for corporate debt and public debt, which in turn induces at least in part increased investment and a larger supply of real assets.
Note also that the total of savings of all national sectors minus total investments in all sectors equals the surplus(+)/deficit(-) on the current account of the balance of payments. In The Netherlands in the ninety's of the 20th century about 20 percent of the current account surplus can be explained from additional (i.e. due to the demographic imbalance) pension savings and this percentage will increase markedly in the coming decades (J.A. Bikker [1996]).

70 Increased international portfolio diversification can have two opposite effects, first it allegedly increases the potential for risk reduction by being less dependent on the performance of the domestic economy. Secondly, growing integration of worldwide

It appears, however, that even if capital is fully mobile, this does not automatically imply that investors actually diversify their portfolios optimally. Instead, they prefer to invest in 'similar' countries such as the EU-15 or OECD-countries ('home-bias'; R. Portes and H. Rey [1999]).

Though investing in emerging markets undoubtedly will be beneficial for both the Western economies and the emerging economies, the size of the benefits would be rather modest[71]. A. Börsch-Supan et al. [2002] suggest more significant effects of capital mobility even if capital flows are restricted to the EU-15 or OECD-countries. German capital exports to all other OECD-countries are projected to amount 7 to 9 percent of GDP by 2020, declining to about 2 percent in 2040.
But there are also risks involved. If a surplus of saving exists, the accompanying balance of payments surplus may lead to an appreciating currency and loss of competitiveness of the national economy. Such loss can be aggravated if aging at the same time puts a downward pressure on labour supply and the return on capital. When in the following period balance of payments deficits arise – savings decline relative to investment – a reversal of capital flows occurs. This may be harmful for the emerging market economies. One percent of equity holdings by institutional investors in Western countries is equivalent to a manifold percentage, 25 or more, of the market capitalization of the emerging economies in Asia and Latin America.

6.3.9 Towards active aging

To face the problems of aging it is increasingly advocated to extend working life beyond the present effective retirement age. In many countries the retirement age will gradually raise in the coming decades and early retirement by exerting financial pressures is made more difficult[72].
But this is only part of the story. Current practices and attitudes of both older workers and their employers are the major barrier to employment of those over 55 years of age. Conventional and preconceived ideas exist with regard to declining productivity with age and the diminishing ability to (re)train older workers ('old

---

financial markets induces higher correlations of capital returns across different geographical areas and thereby reduces the potential for risk reduction.
R. Cragg [1998] tries to answer the question where people from the developed world could invest. Not surprisingly he recommends that investors should switch their funds from OECD to non-OECD countries, as the latter countries experience an increase or only a minimal decline in the size of the workforce in the first half of the 21st century. Opposed to what the cover of the book wants us to believe (detailed) survival guidelines are not given however.

71 H. Blommestein [OECD, 1998], L. MacKellar and H. Reisen [1997] and R. Holzmann [2000].

72 Japan is raising the pensionable age from 60 to 65, incrementally up to 2013. The US will raise it from 65 to 67 years over the next 20 years. In Switzerland, the basic pensionable age for women is being raised from 62 to 65 (the existing age for men) over the period till 2009. Belgium, Portugal and the UK are among the other countries raising pensionable ages of women to those of men.

dogs can not learn new tricks'). In addition, there often is a mismatch of older workers' skills and knowledge and abilities required, unless older workers are ready to accept 'McDonald type' of jobs.
Expanding part-time work is highly recommended to stimulate older workers to remain in the labour force. Shorter working time enables them to escape from the high demands of their prior full-time jobs and to better cope with family responsibilities and personal preferences. Learning throughout a worker's lifetime is one of those recommendations to strengthen the labour market position of older workers. This issue is much discussed, but still insufficiently practised. Little systematic, sustained or large-scale policy action has been taken so far in the developed Western countries in the field of permanent education. Nonetheless, the necessity for lifelong learning will increase, as future labour shortages will arise.
However, the outcome of a range of stimulating measures to increase the labour participation of older workers may be disappointing. For many people retirement at rather young ages is still the preferred status, if income is adequate. Given reasonable economic growth more leisure than today is possible in the future at least from an economic point of view.

Concluding

Major changes are needed in employer and employee attitudes regarding the employment and training of individuals over their life cycle to increase overall work participation.
In respect of the work-leisure choice, we believe that a significant and increasing group of older people exists that wants something else besides ever more leisure and family obligations. The present baby-boom generations are well equipped – they are the best-educated and healthiest generations so far – to undergo the shift towards more active aging. In addition, active aging can contribute to health gain, self-esteem and social contact.

6.4 Long-run trends

Population aging is a long-run process occurring over the same time period as major institutional and technological developments, growth of international trade and globalisation, which will reduce the adverse effects of population aging and favour future economic development. It can be assumed (as we did in the present monograph) that there exists a key trend of a further rise in labour productivity, which may far outweigh the relevance of population aging. Population aging does not operate in isolation. The gloomy short-term perspectives contradict the long-term prospect of global developments and technological change, which favour the international economy[73].

73 According to J.H. Schultz, A. Borowski and W.H. Crown [1991, p. 341], 'Not only is most of "the burden of the elderly" literature is oversimplistic; it encourages us to look for solutions in the wrong places. Today, as in the past, the most important determinants of the future economic welfare of people (of all ages) are the longstanding factors discussed by

Several long-run trends reduce the expected adverse effects of population aging on the economy, the most important of which is the growth of labour productivity. Another major trend is the growing flexibility and decentralization of economic activities, indicated as institutional changes. There is a development from the (post-war) Keynesian economy – characterized by mass production techniques, large national corporations, standardized products, mixed economic order and an extensive welfare state with centralized pension systems – to the capitalist post-industrial society, with ITC-induced smaller-scale production and flexible production techniques, diversified products and less commitments to the former welfare state (L. Laczko and C. Phillipson [1991]). The share of the old industries in total GDP is diminishing.

The formal retirement at a fixed age in the former centralized welfare state hence will evolve in the post-industrial state into a flexible (earlier and partial) exit route at various ages, based on more diversified and to a large extent privatised arrangements, which are predominantly actuarially fair on an individual basis. Institutional innovations in respect of retirement practices – more diversified, less restrictive – will in an atomised society to a major extent solve the problems associated with aging. The new exit routes comply with the new ways of production, the increased welfare of large groups of population and a new balance between individual and collective responsibilities. Growth in labour productivity will do the rest, leaving room for a further increase in welfare. Evidently there appears to be much reliance on market forces with their own merits and demerits.
In this brave new world societies can adapt their economies successfully and can get older comfortably, without creating a burden for any age or population group.

6.4.1 Social cohesion

The more developed countries are faced with crises in their pension and health-care systems not because they are poor, but because by historical and other standards they are extremely rich. The large increase in per capita production and income over the 20th century has made possible that the average length of the retirement period increased fivefold, the proportion of a cohort living to retirement age is about 80 percent – of a male cohort born in 1875 a proportion of only 0.25 or less attained the age of 65 – and the amount of leisure time available to those who are in the labour force increased at least threefold.
Analysts and policy makers now are of the opinion that it is not possible to extend those trends unchanged throughout the 21st century and beyond due to increasing economic and social barriers. The limits to growth come through.

---

economists and others as influencing growth: labour-force participation, saving, investment in human and business capital, technological change, entrepreneurial initiatives, managerial skills, government provision of infrastructure, and so on. Thus the debate over how best to run an economic system is not primarily an aging discussion. In fact, the aging of populations may have little to do with the outcome.'

An aging population is a minor problem compared with a serious disfunctioning of the formal labour market, high inflation, low real capital returns and, above all, low or stagnant productivity growth. In the unlikely (?) event of a widespread economic collapse older people are exposed to serious hardship, but they will not be a cause of the economic fall.
As population ages and pension systems mature the discussion on the balance between contributions paid and benefits received will intensify, giving rise to generational tensions[74]. The worst case scenario is a war of all against all other, 'bellum omnium contra omnes'.

The maintenance of social order and solidarity, social and governmental instability, crime, health and education in many countries nowadays seem to be bigger issues than the problems of aging, though they all have an impact on older people. The mechanisms of social cohesion or generational integration appear to be weakening. Family and community care are becoming less and less evident on a worldwide scale.
In global terms pensions and accessible health care are for the privileged few. At short notice no solutions will be found to the political, social and economic problems of expanding their coverage and raising the level of pensions and care where they are now low.

In less developed countries and in more developed countries as well, older people who have families, therefore, will almost certainly continue to rely on them. Aging societies will face great difficulties if they do not adopt for policies to restore and strengthen social cohesion and stable family structures. Traditional care systems need support by policy makers and governments. New ways of producing family care and social cohesion are urgently needed as in many countries adequate public pension and health care schemes with broad coverage simply do not exist. The discourse in Western countries of elderly people as a burden will not contribute to improve social order and generational integration.

6.4.2 A society for all ages

In the Western aging countries the demographic transition and the related economic and social changes pose huge challenges for policies on aging in various dimensions. First, redesigning pension schemes and early retirement routes, inducing higher labour force participation. Secondly, a reorientation of health care systems from a curative to a preventive model, promoting healthy aging and preventing ill-health and disability and, thirdly, reforming the social security system from supporting dependency to promoting reintegration and stimulating independent life.

---

74 Those tensions can be reinforced by the way (stronger and more self-assured, thereby giving rise to much irritation) the large groups of elderly express their interests.

Summarizing, the policy challenge for government and society is to recognize the relationships between various policy areas, viz. employment, lifelong education and learning, social protection and preventing social exclusion, pensions and retirement, health and long-term care, but also adequate housing and transport and so on. Individuals have a hard duty to take actively advantage of lifelong training and learning, thereby increasing their earning capacity, and to promote their own health and well being over the life course (obligation to healthy lifestyle).
In other words, the comprehensive and effective policy strategy on active aging is based on a partnership between citizens and society. Citizens of all ages and the society will benefit. Both get the best from the investment in human capital, thereby enhancing productivity, increasing labour market and community participation, avoiding intergenerational conflicts and social exclusion, particularly in later life and creating a fairer, more inclusive society[75].

6.4.3 Concluding observations

Reforming pension systems exists in constructing a system that will simultaneously ensure adequate pensions for the current and future pensioners and a viable level of current contributions that will have positive effects on macro-economic variables as saving, investments and public finance. We must fear that political pressures and cultural attitudes will likely produce ill-shaped compromises. The spread of early retirement schemes in virtually all developed countries in the last three decades is an example of bad policy-making.
It has been pointed out by D.C. Muelller [2002] that any proposal for a fundamental reform of the pension system would force a society to contemplate the welfare of present and future generations directly, combined with reformulating present arrangements to provide certain minimum guarantees to all individuals. This also requires that each individual citizen recognizes that the responsibility for his present and future welfare rests not with the state or community, but ultimately with the individual citizen himself.

In respect of the likely consequences of population aging on the performance of the economy pessimistic and optimistic scenarios exist. The pessimistic scenario works like this: population aging means a heavier burden for a smaller working age population to support a twice as large population of inactive elderly. This will inter alia result in lower public and private savings and severe budgetary strains, leading to a slowdown of the economy and lower standards of living for all. The more optimistic scenario relies on the incentives for more investment in human capital. Scarcity of labour relative to physical capital will result in an increase in wages relative to capital returns, which will in turn stimulate investment in human capital and, secondly, promote a rise in labour force participation particularly among those over the age of 55 years. This will contribute to a stronger performance of the

75 A strategy for and a life course perspective on active aging is described by A. Walker [2002]

economy, higher economic growth and higher welfare for all in the medium and long term.

A proviso is that, recognizing the greater opportunities for investment in human capital, we cannot be certain that those investments actually occur.

7 Summarizing and concluding remarks

Ten summarizing and concluding remarks are made.

* The so-called demographic transition primarily results from a decline in fertility rates, followed by increased longevity. Countries over the world are in different phases of the demographic transition. In all more developed countries and in many less developed countries as well over the course of the next 50 years there will be a substantial increase in the proportion of the population of age over 65 and a substantial decrease in the proportion of the population aged under 20. The working age population (those between 20 and 64 years of age) is less increasing or even slightly decreasing in the coming half century. Hence, young people in the developed countries (and in the more rapidly aging developing countries as well) likely will have to pay higher pension contributions, but out of higher incomes, thereby leaving further welfare growth for all. Older people have to work longer, but at better jobs and under better working conditions. Pensioners will receive lower incomes in relative terms and their assets unfortunately will be less worth than they expected.
The demographic transition presents the developed world with marked challenges and the developing world with appealing opportunities.

* Technological change, product specialization on a global scale together with international trade, institutional changes and population aging are all elements of the same long-term process. Hence, future production levels suffice to sustain a twice as large retired population. Society can afford to grow old. Population aging is not likely to create an aggregate shortage of savings and investment, thereby lowering the future resource base. There is more reason to be concerned about a qualified labour supply, notably in the health care sector. Note also that unemployment has reached levels comparable to the size of the elderly population in many Western countries[76]. Thus, there are much more resources that can be used. Policies stimulating labour force participation are necessary. Without sustained improvements in labour productivity and without increases in labour force participation economic growth rates in the EU-15 and in many other countries as well, will slow down in the coming decades.
The central conclusion of several general equilibrium multi-country simulation studies, done by IMF [1991], OECD [1998[b]] and European Commission [1999, 2001, 2002] is that economic growth may slow down as populations age. The studies of the OECD and the European Commission also include calculations of the effect of comprehensive reform scenarios. Their impact is beneficial. They will more than compensate the negative effects associated with aging.

* Though population aging has not proven to be a real constraint on productivity so far, it may nevertheless require major adjustments as to the mechanism of distributing national product, hence to economic and social policies. The main example is the balancing of public budgets in respect of basic pension schemes, health care facilities and other government expenditures on behalf of the elderly. Higher taxes levied on labour income cause distortionary effects, impeding in turn economic development. To avoid budgetary imbalances and distributive problems (generational equity) drastic policy measures have to be taken on a broad front, viz. reducing benefits, increasing contribution rates, raising the retirement age and policies to improve the working of product and factor markets (labour and capital) and the allocation of resources. As a result economic growth will be boosted.

* Though the way of pension financing does not affect in its essentials the distribution across time of the resources to be transferred to the elderly, pay-and-you-go and funding differ in that the former increases labour costs as contributions and payroll taxes are predominantly paid out of workers' income or from the government's budget. There appears to be a strong emphasis upon fiscal and budgetary aspects to the neglect of a probable and hypothetically reasonable projection of real income and productivity growth, provided that adequate policy measures are taken.
To avoid severe fiscal and budgetary imbalances funding as a method of pension finance can be helpful, as reserving pension capital revenues for old age income provisions are not regarded as a burden opposed to contribution payments under a pay-as-you-go system.

* The basic issue in respect of accrued pension rights is that it constitutes a claim on future output in exchange for foregoing a part of present output. The real value of that claim under both systems depends on the availability of future resources. Under funding this value is dependent on e.g. inflationary processes, capital returns and the (market) price of assets. Under pay-as-you-go the claim value depends on the ability and the willingness of workers and taxpayers to finance pension outlays. Pensioners need and have under funding a firm and solid claim on national product, arising from their identifiable ownership of productive capital as a resource base of their own. Production is the result of the joint input of labour (belonging to the younger generations) and capital (to a large extent belonging to the elderly). Hence, pensions can be paid out of capital revenues rather than out of the labour income of the next generation.

* If funding of pension provision makes little difference as it does not increase national savings, investments and therefore does not lead to a higher national product, all aging countries may have similar problems ahead. It is often

76 The EU opposed to the US and Japan, has still considerable unemployment. The paradox is that this weakness represents at the same time its force in facing the demographic transition.

argued that the pension systems in e.g. France, Germany and Italy are not sustainable in the coming decades. Note, however, that saving rates and capital formation are not lower in the aforementioned countries than in the UK and the US.

If funding is (a part of) the solution, countries like Switzerland, the Netherlands and the UK are (happily) faced with a problem that can be easier dealt with than that in the aforementioned continental countries. From a security point of view, the UK pension system is (for the retirees) preferential to the systems we find in France, Germany and Italy. Nonetheless there is no bigger pie available out of which larger slices can be given. Guarantees are in some way or other always virtual. In a pay-as-you-go scheme they are based on the strength of the implicit social contract between generations, under funding they are based on the ability of the economy always to yield an adequate return on financial assets.

* Particularly imbalances may arise in two situations, one of which is budgetary and the other one originates from an inflationary environment. First, pension schemes predominantly based on pay-as-you-go will lead to a doubling (or more) of contribution rates on labour income. All pension costs are borne by the working population – capital income due to its mobility can not be taxed effectively –, leading to i.a. social injustice and impeding the proper functioning of the labour market. Second, when asset prices fall as pensioners want to sell their assets to the less numerous younger generations, the elderly are left with pension incomes lower than they had expected. Demographic transitions can have significant asset market effects that hit some generations harder than others. The situation might worsen when tight labour markets and fiscal imbalances give rise to inflation.

On the other hand, high capital returns create a world characterized by a large retired leisure class of elderly and a poor working population giving rise to severe social imbalances. It may be concluded that society has more important priorities than allocating ever-increasing parts of national product to sustain an increasing number of ever-wealthier elderly.

* Population aging will change the balance between capital and labour in the developed countries. Labour supply will be scarce whereas capital will be relatively abundant. This will result in higher wages relative to the rate of return to capital. The impact of aging on productivity is highly speculative; opinions widely differ. Increased labour force participation will lessen the wage increase. An adequate albeit modest growth of productivity up to certain degree can compensate for labour scarceness and, hence adverse effects on the economy will be virtually absent. In developing countries the population age structure is younger and their economies are still characterized by a high supply of labour and a low supply of capital in relative terms. As a result, the rate of return on capital is higher in many developing countries. Capital exports to (well selected) developing economies can be helpful to resolve the aging problem in developed countries by shifting production of (consumer) goods to those emerging economies. Political,

social and economic stability are utmost important conditions that have to be met if the demographic dividend were to be reaped.

* A variety of fiscal and other structural measures must be pursued to strengthen the foundations of the economy in coping with the aging in the more developed countries. Gloomy long run projections will actually become optimistic if between now and 2050 a) about 1½ percent (or more) productivity growth can be achieved, b) public pensions and public health expenditures to GDP ratios rise only moderately; an increase of three to five percentage points of GDP should not necessarily be considered as harmful and thus, unacceptable, let alone dramatic, c) budget deficits can be avoided, d) saving ratios and investment levels do not decline and e) we experience a further rise in labour force participation.
Apart from being inpractical immigration in general is dissuaded as the costs often outweigh the benefits. Selective immigration, though detrimental to the country of origin, will be advantageous.
By implementing the right combination of economic and social policy measures with many feedback mechanisms, the adverse effects of population aging on the economy can be adequately compensated for. A fortiori, we could surprise ourselves afterwards by having created a stronger economy in an older society.

* Though welfare increases substantially for all in the coming decades, taxpayers may lose in relative terms due to higher contribution payments associated with aging. It is argued that this is not something to be too concerned about. As individuals continue to grow more affluent, it seems likely that they will spend more on pension provision, health and long-term care, as they earlier did in respect of expenditures for food. Workers of all ages pay more and older workers stay longer in the labour force ('active aging'). Early retirement is strongly discouraged.
Furthermore, societies (urgently) need a new concept of intergenerational commitment. Twentieth century's forms of mandatory solidarity have to be replaced by new forms of generational cultural integration. A central policy objective throughout the world should be to restore and strengthen social cohesion and stable family structures.

Abstract

On Global Aging; old-age income systems in the EU and other major parts of the world

Population aging was unknown before the middle of the 20th century. Nowadays developed countries are in unprecedented transition to a new era with aging populations. Aging will result in a smaller proportion of the population being employed in the decades after 2010/2020. Another primary issue which may harm industrialized economies is whether aging and particularly pay-as-you-go based pension systems will depress saving and investment.

Changing demography, fewer workers and more retirees, gives rise to much concern on the fiscal sustainability of public pension schemes, health care systems and other social services. As a result pension reform is in discussion in all developed countries. The main features of the debate of the relationships between population aging, labour supply and saving behaviour are summarized.*

Technological development, economic globalisation and institutional changes are long-term processes occurring over the same time period as population aging and they are of major and decisive influence.
Under the rather optimistic assumptions of some further increase in labour force participation ratios and that 1¾ percent yearly growth in per worker production can be realized in the coming half century, it can be demonstrated that per capita consumption of the working age population in the EU-15 increases from 2000 to 2020 by 44.7 percent and that of the 65^{+}-population by 81 percent. Without aging welfare in the EU-15 by 2020 would have been 4.2 percent higher.
Only with a zero growth rate of labour productivity average welfare will decrease by about 6 percent in 2020, whereas a minor 0.3 percent productivity growth with unchanged labour participation rate suffices to maintain welfare at its present level. On the other hand, a desired per capita welfare increase of e.g. 60 percent over the period 2000-2020 requires an annual productivity growth rate of 2¼ percent.

Economic growth under aging is not an automatic process. To achieve higher welfare growth well chosen packages of reform policy measures are necessary, primarily directed at providing incentives for people to invest in their human capital and to stimulate labour force participation. Increasing scarcity of labour

---

* The concern about aging is briefly summarized by Donald J. Johnston, secretary-general of the OECD, '. the aging of our societies over coming decades present OECD-countries with a complex and formidable set of interrelated challenges', preface of OECD [1998a].

relative to physical capital and subsequent higher wage levels make such shifts also more attractive. It is shown conclusively that the aging of the population needs not give rise to a slowdown of the economy. It is not demography but economic growth rates that determine the nature of old-age income systems in the 21st century.

References

Aaron, H.J (1982): Economic effects of social security. The Brookings Institution, Washington, D.C.

Aaron, H.J., Bosworth, B.P., G. Burtless (1989): Can America afford to grow old?, paying for social security. The Brookings Institution, Washington, D.C.

Alessie, R.J.M., Kapteyn, A., Klijn, F. (1997): Mandatory pensions and personal savings in the Netherlands. De Economist 45, 1997, 291-324.

Auerbach, A.J., Kotlikoff, L.J. (1987): Dynamic Fiscal Policy. Cambridge University Press, Cambridge, MA.

Auerbach, A.J., Kotlikoff, L.J., Hageman, P.R., Nicoletti, G. (1989): The economic dynamics of an aging population: the case of four OECD countries. OECD Economic Studies no. 12, 97-130.

Barr, N. (2000): Reforming pensions: myths, truths, and policy choices. Working Paper no. 00/39, International Monetary Fund, Washington, D.C..

Bikker, J.A. (1996): National savings, the current account and aging populations: a pension fund model. Economic and Financial Modelling 3, 1-20.

Blommestein, H. (1998): Ageing-induced capital flows to emerging markets do not solve the basic pension problem in the OECD area. Financial Market Trends no. 70. OECD, Paris, 83-94.

Blöndal, S., Scarpetta, S. (1999): The retirement decision in OECD countries. Economics Department Working Paper no. 202, OECD, Paris.

Bloom, D.E., Canning, D., Sevilla, J. (2001): Economic growth and the demographic transition. Working Paper no. 8685, NBER, Washington D.C.

Bohn, H. (1999): Social security and demographic uncertainty: the risk sharing properties of alternative policies. Working Paper no. 7030, NBER, Cambridge.

Börsch-Supan, A. (1996): The impact of population aging on savings, investment and growth in the OECD area. In: Future global capital shortages: real threat or pure fiction, OECD, Paris, 103-142.

Börsch-Supan, A. (1998): Germany, a social security system on the verge of collapse. In: Siebert, H. (ed.): Redesigning Social Security, Mohr Siebeck, Tübingen, 129-160.

Börsch-Supan, A. (2001): Labor market effects of population aging. Working Paper no. 8640, NBER, Washington D.C.

Börsch-Supan, A., Winter, J.K. (2001): Population aging, savings behaviour and capital markets. Working Paper no. 8561, NBER, Washington D.C.

Börsch-Supan, A., Ludwig, A., Winter, J.K. (2002): Aging and international capital flows. In: Auerbach, A.J., Herrmann, H. (eds.): Ageing, Financial Markets and Monetary Policy. Springer, Heidelberg, 191-227.

Bosworth, B. (1996): Prospects for saving and investment in industrial countries. In: Future global capital shortages: real threat or pure fiction, OECD, Paris, 19-46.

Bosworth, B.,G. Burtless, G. (1998): Aging societies, the global dimension. Brookings Institution Press, Washington D.C.

Bovenberg, A.L. and A.S.M. van der Linden, A.S.M. (1997): Can we afford to grow old?. CPB research memorandum no. 134, The Hague.

Bovenberg, A.L. (2002): Pension systems in aging societies. In: Siebert, H. (ed.): Economic Policy for Ageing Societies. Springer, Heidelberg, 183-206.

Breyer, F. (1990): Ökonomische Theorie der Altersicherung. Verlag Franz Vahlen, München.

Broer, D.P. (2001): Growth and welfare distribution in an aging society: an applied general equilibrium analysis for the Netherlands. De Economist 149, 81-114.

Broer, D.P., Westerhout, E.W.M.T. (1996): Pension policies and lifetime uncertainty in an applied general equilbrium model. In: Broer, D.P., Lassila, J. (eds.): Pension policies and public debt in dynamic CGE models. Physica Verlag, Heidelberg, 110-125.

Brooks, R. (2000[a]): Life cycle portfolio choice and asset market effects of the baby boom, Research Paper, IMF, Washington, D.C.

Brooks, R. (2000[b]): Population aging and global capital flows in a parallel universe. Working Paper no. 151, IMF, Washington, D.C.

Chand, S.K., Jaeger, A. (1996): Aging populations and public pension schemes. Occasional Paper no. 147, IMF, Washington D.C.

Chauveau, T., Loufir, R. (1997): The future of public pensions in the seven major economies. In: Broer, D.P., Lassila, J. (eds.): Pension policies and public debt in dynamic CGE models. Physica Verlag, Heidelberg, 16-73.

CPB (1996): Omgevingsscenario's Lange Termijn Verkenning 1995-2020. Working Paper no. 89, The Hague.

CPB/CBS (1997): Bevolking en arbeidsaanbod, drie scenario's tot 2020. SDU, The Hague.

CPB (2000): Ageing in the Netherlands, SDU, The Hague.

Cutler, D.M., Poterba, J.M., Sheiner, L.M., Summers, L.H. (1990): An aging society: opportunity or challenge? Brookings Papers on Economic Activity 1, 1-73.

Dang, T.-T., Antolin, P., Oxley, H. (2001): Fiscal implications of ageing: projections of age-related spending. Economics Department Working Paper no. 305, OECD, Paris.

Davis, E.P. (1998[a]): European pensions, 'fundamental' influences and the role of Economic and Monetary Union. Journal of Pensions Management & Marketing 3, 206-237.

Davis, E.P. (1998[b]): Population aging and retirement income provision in the European Union. In: Bosworth, B., Burtless, G. (eds.): Ageing Societies. Brookings Institution Press, Washington, D.C., 33-110.

Davis, E.P. (2002): Ageing and financial stability. In: Auerbach, A.J., Herrmann, H. (eds.): Ageing, Financial Markets and Monetary Policy. Springer, Heidelberg, 191-227.

Diamond, P.A. (1997): Insulation of pensions from political risk. In: Valdés-Prieto, S. (ed.): The economics of pensions, principles, policies, and international experience. Cambridge University Press, Cambridge, 33-57.

Dielen, H., Kalshoven, C., Schotsman, H. (2002): Nog vele jaren! ABN-AMRO, Amsterdam.

Disney, R. (1996): Can we afford to grow older; a perspective on the economics of aging. MIT Press, Cambridge, MA.

Disney, R. (2000): Crises in public pension programmes in OECD: what are the reform options? The Economic Journal 110, 1-23.

Disney, R., Johnson, P. (eds.): Pension systems and retirement incomes across OECD countries. Edward Elgar, Cheltenham, UK.

Economic Policy Committee/EU (2000): Progress report to the Ecofin Council on the impact of ageing populations on public pension systems, Brussels.

Economic Policy Committee/EU (2001): Budgetary challenges posed by ageing populations: the impact on public spending on pensions, health and long-term care for the elderly and possible indicators of the long-term sustainability of public finances, Brussels.

Economic Policy Committee/EU (2002): Reform challenges facing public pension systems; the impact of certain parametric reforms on pension expenditure, Brussels.

Elmeskov, J., Scarpetta, S. (2000): New sources of economic growth in Europe?, 28th economic conference of the Österreichische Nationalbank, OECD, Paris.

Engen, E.M., Gale, W.G. (1997): Effects of social security reform on private and national saving. In: Sass, S.A. and Triest, R.K. (eds.): Social security reforms; links to saving, investment and growth. Conference Proceedings, Federal reserve bank of Boston, Boston.

Englander, A.S., Gurney, A. (1994): OECD productivity growth: medium-term trends OECD Economic Studies no 22, 112-130.

Esping-Andersen, G., Duncan, G., Hemerijck, A., Myles, J. (2001): A new welfare architecture for Europe? Report submitted to the Belgian Presidency of the European Union, Brussels.

European Commission (1999), see McMorrow, K., Roeger, W. (1999).

European Commission (2001): Prospects and policy challenges for the EU economy. Brussels, 2001.

European Commission (2002), see McMorrow, K., Roeger, W. (2002).

European Round Table of Industrialists (2000): European Pensions, an appeal for reform. Brussels.

Euwals, R. (2000): Do mandatory pensions decrease household savings?, evidence for the Netherlands. De Economist 148, 643-670.

Fair, R.C., Dominguez, K.M. (1991): Effects of the changing US age distribution on macroeconomic equations. American Economic Review 81, 1276-1294.

Feldstein, M.S. (1974): Social security, induced retirement and aggregate capital formation. Journal of Political Economy 82, 905-926.

Feldstein, M.S. (1995): Social security and saving: new time series evidence. Working Paper no. 5054, NBER, Washington, D.C.

Feldstein, M.S., Siebert, H. (eds.) (2002): Social security pension reform in Europe, University of Chicago Press, Chicago.

Fenge, R. (1995): Pareto-efficiency of the pay-as-you-go pension system with intergenerational fairness. Finanzarchiv 52, 357-363.

Ferguson, N., Kotlikoff, L.J. (2000): The degeneration of EMU. Foreign Affairs 79, 101-121.

Fougère, M., Mérette, M. (1997): Population ageing and economic growth in seven OECD countries. Ministry of Finance of Canada, Ottawa.

Franco, D., Munzi, T. (1996): Public pension expenditure prospects in the European Union: a survey of national projections. In: European Economy, European Commission, Brussels.

Franssen, W. (2002): Increased labour force participation among older people: Holland's trump card in countering the effects of an ageing population. In: Social security and changes in the world of work. ISSA, Geneva, 133-144.

Futagami, K., Nakajima, T. (2001): Population aging and economic growth. Journal of Macroeconomics 23, 31-44.

Gern, K.-J., (2001): Recent developments in old-age pension systems - an international overview. In: Feldstein, M., Siebert, H. (eds.): Social security pension reforms in Europe. University of Chicago Press, Chicago, 439-478.

Group of Ten (1998): The macroeconomic and financial implications of ageing populations. Bank for International Settlements, Basle.

Hebbink, G.E. (1996): Vergrijzing, overheidsfinancien en besparingen: een overzicht van recente literatuur (in Dutch). Maandschrift Economie 60, 407-430.

Heller, P. et al. (1986): Aging and social expenditures in the major industrial countries, 1980-2025. Occasional Paper no. 47, IMF, Washington, D.C.

Hemming, R. (1999): Should public pensions be funded? International Social Security Review 52/1, 3-30.

Henkens, C.J.I.M. (1998): Older workers in transition; studies in the early retirement decisions in the Netherlands. NIDI, The Hague.

Heyma, A.O.H. (1990): Dynamic models of retirement from the labour force: an empirical analysis of early exit in the Netherlands. Leyden University Press, Leiden.

Higgins, R. (1999): Demography, national savings and international capital flows. International Economic Review 39, 532-574.

Hillman, A.L. (2002): Immigration and intergenerational transfers. In: Siebert, H. (ed.): Economic Policy for Ageing Societies. Springer, Heidelberg, 213-226.

Holzmann, R. (2000): Can investments in emerging markets help to solve the aging problem? Social Protection Discussion Paper no. 00/010, World Bank, Washington D.C..

Hughes, G., Stewart, J. (eds.) (2000): Pension in the European Union: adapting to economic and social change. Kluwer, Boston.

Hviding, K., Mérette, M. (1998): Macroeconomic effects of pension reforms in the context of ageing populations: overlapping generations model simulations for seven OECD-countries. Economics Department Working Paper no. 201, OECD, Paris.

IBRD (World Bank) (1994): Averting the old-age crisis; policies to protect the old and promote growth. Oxford University Press, Oxford.

ILO (2000): Social security pensions; development and reform. Geneva.

IMF (1990): see Masson, P.R. and R.W. Tryon (1990).

INGENUE-team (Aglietta, M., Arezki, R., Breton, R., Fayolle, J., Juillard, M., Lacu, C., Cacheux, J. Le, Rzepkowsky, B., Touzé, V.) (2002): Macroeconomic consequences of pension reforms in Europe: an investigation with the INGENUE world model. CEPII-CEPREMAP-OFCE, Paris.

Jacobzone, S., Cambois, E., Robine, J.-M. (2000): Is the health of older persons in OECD countries improving fast enough to compensate for population ageing? OECD Economic Studies no. 30, Paris.

JETRO (Japan External Trade Organization) (2001): Comparison of systems in Japan, US, Western Europe and Asia, paper 2nd Policy Summit of the Global Aging Initiative (Zürich, January 2001), Tokyo.

Johnson, P., Zimmermann, K.F. (eds.) (1993): Labour markets in an ageing Europe. Cambridge University Press, Cambridge.

Johnson, P. (2002): The impact of ageing: the supply of labour and human capital. In: Siebert, H. (ed.): Economic Policy for Ageing Societies. Springer, Heidelberg, 111-125.

Jousten, A., Pestieau, P. (2001): Labor mobility, redistribution and pension reform in Europe. In: Feldstein, M., Siebert, H. (eds.): Social security pension reforms in Europe. University of Chicago Press, Chicago, 2001.

Kandiyoti, D. (1999): Poverty in transition: an ethnographic critique of household surveys in post-Soviet Central Asia. Development and Change 30, 499-524.

Kinsella, K., Velkoff, V.A. (both from US Census Bureau) (2001): An aging world. US Government Printing Office, Washington, D.C.

Kohl, R., O'Brien, P. (1998): The macroeconomics of ageing, pensions and savings: a survey, Economics Department Working Paper no. 200, OECD, Paris.

Kotlikoff, L.J., Smetters, K., Walliser, J. (2001): Finding a way out of America's demographic dilemma. Working Paper no. 8258, NBER, Cambridge, MA.

Kuné, J.B. (2000): Issues in Pension Finance. Netherlands Foundation for Pension Studies. The Hague.

Laczko, F., Phillipson, C. (1991): Changing work and retirement; social policy and the older worker. Open University Press, Milton Keynes.

Leibfritz, W., Roseveare, D., Fore, D., Wurzel, E. (1996): Aging populations, pension systems and government budgets: how do they affect saving? In: Future global capital shortages: real threat or pure fiction, OECD, Paris, 47-102.

Lichtenberg, F.R. (2002): Sources of U.S. longevity increase, 1960-1997. Working Paper no. 8755, NBER, Washington D.C.

Liedtke, P.M. (2001): Driving potential pension solutions. Working Paper, Geneva Association, Geneva.

Lindeboom, M. (1998): Microeconometric analysis of the retirement decision: the Netherlands. Economics Department Working Paper no. 207, OECD, Paris.

Liu, S., MacKellar, L. (2001): Key issues of aging and social security in China. Interim Report no. 4, IIASA, Laxenburg.

MacKellar, L., Reisen, H. (1997): A simulation model of global pension fund investment. Research Paper, OECD, Paris.

MacKellar, L., Ermolieva, T., Horlacher, D., Mayhew, L. (2002): Economic impacts of population aging in Japan. IIASA, Laxenburg.

MacManus, S.A. (1996): Young v. Old, generational combat in the 21st century. Westview Press, Boulder, Co.

Mantel, J. (1999): European Pension Reforms; three fundamental questions. Merrill Lynch, London.

Masson, P.R., Tryon, R.W. (1990): Macroeconomic effects of projected population aging in industrial countries,. IMF Staff Papers 37, 453-485.

Masson, P.R. (1991): Effects of long-run demographic changes in a multi-country model. IMF Working Paper no. 91/123, Washington, D.C.

McMorrow, K., Roeger, W. (1999): The economic consequences of ageing populations. Economic Papers no. 138, DG for economic and financial affairs/European Commission, Brussels.

McMorrow, K., Roeger, W. (2002): EU pension reform – an overview of the debate and an empirical assessment of the main policy reform options. Economic Papers no.162, DG for economic and financial affairs/European Commission, Brussels.

Michalski, W., Miller, R., Stevens, B. (1995): Future global capital shortages; some key issues and policy recommendations. In: Future global capital shortages: real threat or pure fiction, OECD, Paris, 7-18.

Miles, D. (1997): Financial markets, ageing and social welfare. Fiscal Studies 18, 161-187.

Miles, D. (1999): Modelling the impact of demographic change on the economy. The Economic Journal 109, 1-36.

Miles, D. (2002[a]): The influence of ageing on capital accumulation. In: Siebert, H. (ed.): Economic Policy for Ageing Societies. Springer, Heidelberg, 131-154.

Miles, D. (2002[b]): Should monetary policy be different in a greyer world? In: Auerbach, A.J., Herrmann, H. (eds.): Ageing, Financial Markets and Monetary Policy. Springer, Heidelberg, 243-276.

Mueller, D.C. (2002): The political economy of aging societies, In: Siebert, H. (ed.): Economic Policy for Ageing Societies. Springer, Heidelberg, 269-284.

Mullan, P. (2000): The imaginary time bomb, why an aging population is not a social problem. I.B. Tauris, Londòn.

Nimwegen, N., Beets, G. (2000): Bevolkingsvraagstukken in Nederland anno 2000 (in Dutch). NIDI, The Hague.

Roseveare, D., Leibfritz, W., Fore, D. Wurzel, E. (1996): Ageing populations, pension systems and government budgets: simulations for 20 OECD countries. Working Paper no. 168, OECD, Paris.

OECD (1996): Ageing in OECD countries, a critical policy challenge. Paris.

OECD (1998[a]): Maintaining prosperity in an ageing society. Paris.

OECD (1998[b]): see Turner, D. et al. (1998).

OECD (2000[a]): Reforms for an Ageing Society. Paris.

OECD (2001): Links between policy and growth: cross-country evidence. Economic Outlook no. 68, OECD, Paris.

OECD (2001): Fiscal implications of ageing: projections of age-related spending. Economic Outlook no. 69, OECD, Paris.

OECD (2001): Aging and income; financial resources and retirement in 9 OECD countries. OECD, Paris.

Oksanen, H. (2002): Pension reforms: key issues illustrated with an actuarial model. Economic Papers no. 174, DG for economic and financial affairs/European Commission, Brussels.

Peterson, P.G. (1999): Gray dawn; how the coming age wave will transform America – and the world. Times Book, New York.

Portes, R., Rey, H. (1999): The determinants of cross-border equity flows. Working Paper no. 7336, NBER, Washington D.C.

Poterba, J.M. (1998): Population age structure and asset returns: an empirical investigation. Working Paper no. 6774, NBER, Washington D.C.

Poterba, J.M., Venti, S.F., Wise, D.A. (1998): Personal retirement saving programs and asset accumulation: reconciling the evidence. In: Wise, D.A. (ed.): Frontiers in the Economics of Aging. University of Chicago Press, Chicago.

Reinhardt, U.E. (2002): Health care for the aging baby boomers: how serious a problem? In: Siebert, H. (ed.): Economic Policy for Aging Societies. Springer, Heidelberg, 235-262.

Roseveare, D., Leibfritz, W., Fore, D., Wurzel, E. (1996): Ageing populations, pension systems and government budgets: simulations for 20 OECD-countries. Working Paper no. 168, OECD, Paris.

Schieber, S.J., Shoven, J.B. (1997): The consequences of population aging on private pension fund saving and asset markets. In: Schieber, S.J., Shoven, J.B. (eds.): Public policies towards pensions. MIT Press, Cambridge, MA, 219-246.

Schultz, J.H., Borowski, A., Crown, W.H. (1991): Economics of population aging, the "graying" of Australia, Japan and the United States. Auburn House, New York, 1991.

Siebert, H. (ed.) (1998): Redesigning social security. Mohr Siebeck, Tübingen.

Sociale Verzekeringsbank (2001): Grenzen aan de premie (in Dutch). Economisch-Statistische Berichten, D8-9.

Spillman, B.C., Lubitz, L. (2000): The effect of longevity on spending for acute and long-term care. New England Journal of Medicine 342, 1409-1415.

Stowe England, R. (2002): The fiscal challenge of an aging industrial world, CSIS, Washington, DC.

Stowe England, R. (2002): Global aging and financial markets; hard landings ahead?, CSIS, Washington, DC.

Stowe England, R. (2002): The macroeconomic impact of global aging, CSIS, Washington, DC.

Thompson, L.H. (1995): The advantages and disadvantages of different social welfare strategies. International Social Security Review 48, 59-73.

Thompson, L.H. (1996): Principles of financing social security pensions. International Social Security Review 49, 45-63.

Thompson, L.H. (1998): Older and wiser: the economics of public pensions. The Urban Institute Press, Washington, D.C.

Tinker, M., Nossek, V., Elgeti, R., O'Sullivan, M. (2002): Pension reforms in Europe; Europes' Enron: implications for equities, bonds and alternative investments. Commerzbank, Frankfurt.

Turner, D., Giorno, C., De Serres, A., Vourc'h, A., Richardson, P. (1998): The macroeconomic implications of ageing in a global context. Economics Department Working Paper no. 193, OECD, Paris.

UN (2000): Replacement migration: is it a solution to declining and ageing populations? UN Population Division, New York.

Vandenbroucke, F. (2001): Sustainable social justice through European coordination? Tinbergen lecture, Koninklijke Vereniging voor de Staatshuishoudkunde, Amsterdam.

Vandenbroucke, F. (2002): Social justice and open coordination in Europe, reflections on Drèze's Tinbergen lecture. De Economist 150, 2002, 83-93.

Vatter, H.G., Walker, J.F. (1998): Support for baby-boom retirees - not to worry. Journal of Economic Issues 32, 79-86.

Visco, I. (2001): Economic policy for aging societies. Conference Paper, OECD, Paris.

Walker, A., Naegele, G.(eds.) (1999): The politics of old age in Europe. Open University Press, Buckingham.

Walker, A. (2002): A strategy for active ageing. International Social Security Review 55(1), 121-139.

Wallace, P. (1999): Agequake, riding the demographic rollercoaster shaking business, finance and our world. Nicholas Brealey Publishing, London.

Wigger, B.U. (2002): Public Pensions and Economic growth. Springer, Heidelberg.

World Bank, see IBRD.

Appendix A. Methodology

A1 Methodology

In this section the Dutch demography is taken as an explanatory case for the methodology used. Assume that, in the benchmark year 2000, the per capita consumption of persons aged 20-64 is 100, that of young ones (mostly children) 50 and that the consumption level of older people is still lagging behind somewhat at 80 (Table A1). Hence, total consumption in the baseline year is 8516. Ignoring investments and a surplus or shortage on the (current account of the) balance of payments, the volume of production also amounts to 8516. That is 193.0 per worker.

In the baseline scenario it is assumed that 1¾ percent yearly growth rate in per worker production can be realized in the coming decades and that the labour force participation ratio in the Netherlands increases from 0.71 in 2000 to 0.77 in 2020.

Per capita consumption is a measure of personal welfare. Total consumption expenditures are a stable share of total national output[1]. Under these assumptions the proportion of gross domestic product (GDP) allocated for personal consumption expenditures – in 2020 amounting to 13639 – which enables an average per capita consumption of 141.7 for all people over 20 years of age (Table A1). Note that in 2020 equal consumption opportunities exist for the active population and the elderly. The end of the struggle for emancipation is attained.
Consumption of the active population increases in the period 2000 to 2020 by 41.7 percent and that of the 65^{+}-population by 77 percent (from index 80 to index 141.7).
In an unchanged population (no aging from 2000 onwards) per capita consumption in the Netherlands would be 151.1 for all people over 20 years of age instead of 141.7. The difference (of 9.4) between the indexes 151.1 and 141.7 can be considered as the consumption sacrifice or the volume of consumptional expenditures forgone by the younger population groups in favour of the elderly.

---

1 Estimates of GDP and GDP growth are also estimates of consumption expenditures and its growth and hence of the growth of personal welfare, albeit the value of consumption of leisure time should also be taken into account.
To demonstrate whether the economies of the more developed countries have the prospective resources to permit (early) retirement, expanded health care and expanded other types of government expenditures, the focus in the present analysis is on the average producer and the average consumer. Three age groups are distinguished. This is a marked simplification – to overcome the frustrating sterility that everything depends on every thing else –, thereby disregarding the dynamic economics on a meso or intermediate level and at a micro or personal level.

Table A1. Production and welfare in the Netherlands in the years 2000, 2020 and 2050 (indexes[1]) for different population cohorts, 0-19y, 20-64y and 65⁺ years of age, assuming 1¾ percent yearly production growth and a labour force participation rate of 0.77 from 2020 onwards opposed to 0.71 in 2000 (demographic projection US Census Bureau)

Age	Population (mln.)	Working-population	C/population	Y/working-population	C(=Y)
(1)	(2)	(3)	(4)	(5)	(6)
2000 (*present time*)					
0-19	24.2	-	50	-	1211
20-64	62.1	44.1	100	193,0	6214
65+	13.7	-	80	-	1092
total	**100.0**	**44.1**	ave. **85.2**	**total 8516**	**8516**
2020 (medium term)					
0-19	22.5	-	70.9	-	1591
20-64	63.8	49.2	141.7	277.5	9045
65+	21.2	-	141.7	-	3003
total	**107.5**	**49.2**	**ave. 126.9**	**total 13639**	**13639**
2050 (long term)					
0-19	20.8	-	107.5		2231
20-64	56.7	43.6	215.0	466.9	12181
65+	27.7	-	215.0	-	5962
total	**105.2**	**43.6**	**ave. 193.8**	**total 20374**	**20374**

1) C is consumption and Y is a part of gross national product

Or, in other words, welfare in the Netherlands in 2020 is 9.4 percent lower than it otherwise without aging would have been.
Between 2020 and 2050 per capita consumption according to rather optimistic assumptions in respect of labour productivity increase with 1.4 percent annually from 141.7 to 215.

A2 Participation rates

All counties are projected to have increasing participation ratios as a result of assumed higher female participation, lower unemployment and increased average retirement age. The effect is stronger (a catch-up is allowed) in countries with currently relatively low female participation (Italy, Spain, the Netherlands and Japan), high unemployment (Spain, Italy, France, Belgium and Eastern European countries) at the beginning of the period. The largest overall increase is 7.3 percentage points in Italy, followed by Spain and Belgium with 6.8 and 6.2 points respectively. There is room for a further increase of the female labour force participation.
Sweden and the UK experience the lowest increase in labour force participation by 1.8 and 2.7 percentage points respectively. Participation ratios are allowed to converge to a highest value of 0.78.
The adverse effects of the aging of the working-age population can to a large extent or even fully be compensated for by an upward adjustment of the effective retirement age. In the second half of the 20th century life expectancy in developed countries increased by about 10 years, whereas retirement age has fallen to below and sometimes far below the age of 60.

The proportion of people in the labour force in the EU-15 hardly changed the last 40 years. The US by contrast experienced a 12 to 13 percentage points increase in participation from 1960 to 2000. The EU-15 has much ground to make up.
In the US, Canada and Japan participation rates are already high at the beginning of the projection period. There is no or hardly any room for a further rise.
In the less developed countries the over-all participation ratios are roughly set at 0.70 in 2000 and are arbitrarily slightly increased to 0.75 by 2020 and 2050. Clearly not availability of labour, but labour productivity is the real issue in the developing world.
Finally note that in comparing participation rates the length of average working week differs among countries.

A3 Observations on the labour force participation of elderly people

The rate of labour force participation of older people varies substantially among countries, and generally is markedly lower in developed countries than in developing countries. Less than 10 percent of men aged 65 and over participate in the labour force in developed countries – Japan stands out with 35.5 percent in the late 1990's, whereas in most developing countries well over half of the elderly men are economically active.

In developed countries labour force participation of men aged 55 and over sharply declined in the last three decades. In the early 1970's about half of men aged 60 to 64 were still active. By the turn of the century only Japan, New Zealand, Sweden and the US had male participation rates over 50 percent. Most European countries were far below with 20 percent or less up to 30 percent. Of men 55 to 59 years of age 50 percent to 90 percent is still in the labour force in the late 1990's, varying among countries from 45.9 percent in Hungary, 52.4 percent in Belgium, 54.1 percent in Italy, 70.4 percent in France, 76.5 percent in Germany, 78.4 percent in the US and as high as 94.7 percent in Japan.
The trend for older women differs from that of men. Female participation rates have increased for all adult age groups up to age 60. Rates for elderly women of 60 years and over like those for men have declined in the last three decades in developed countries.

In developing countries the proportion of economically active elderly people is much higher than in developed countries, and is varying between 80 percent and 90 percent for the male age group 55-59, between 50 percent and 70 percent for the age group 60 to 64 and declining to roughly 50 percent for men of age 65 and over. Labour force participation, though hard to measure, of women in developing countries is also higher than in developed countries, but tends to be lower than for men. In addition, older women are more likely than older men to work in part-time activities.
Not surprisingly, agriculture is by far the most common activity for older workers in developing countries, and rather important also in many developed countries during the last decades of the 20th century.

Table A2. Labour force participation rate in more developed countries, EU-15, US Canada and Japan, Russia and Eastern European countries and less developed countries in the years 2020 and 2050

Year Country (1)	2000 (2)	2020 (3)	2050 (4)	2050 (ultimate target) (5)
EU-15	**0.69**	**0.75**	**0.75**	**0.78**
Belgium	0,638	0.70	0.70	0.78
France	0.682	0.73	0.73	0.78
Germany	0.711	0.75	0.75	0.78
Italy	0.597	0.67	0.67	0.78
Netherlands	0.71	0.77	0.77	0.78
Spain	0.642	0.71	0.71	0.78
Sweden	0.762	0.78	0.78	0.78
UK	0.757	0.78	0.78	0.78
Other developed world				
US	0.783	0.78	0.78	0.78
Canada	0.77	0.78	0.78	0.78
Japan	0.782	0.78	0.78	0.78

Table A2. (continued)

Year Country (1)	2000 (2)	2020 (3)	2050 (4)	2050 (ultimate target) (5)
Eastern European countries				
Russia	0.70	0.75	0.75	0.78
Ukraine	0.70	0.75	0.75	0.78
Poland	0.69	0.75	0.75	0.78
Czech Republic	0.80	0.80	0.80	0.78
Romania	0.70	0.75	0.75	0.78
Hungary	0.60	0.70	0.70	0.78
Other less developed countries				
	0.70	0.75	0.75	0.78

Appendix B. Alternative scenarios

Growth in labour productivity in European countries in the seventies and eighties of the 20th century – a period with rather low productivity growth, but still higher than in the nineties – amounted to 2 percent per year approximately (Englander, A.S. and A. Gurney [1994]). It seems to be reasonable, therefore, to take the productivity growth in these decades as a lower bound for future productivity growth.
On the other hand in the face of feasible negative consequences of population aging on labour supply, labour productivity and saving/investment decisions as well as the falling of the productivity growth due to an aging working population and a higher part of services in national product, that 2 percent productivity growth rate, particularly after 2020, must more likely be considered as an upper bound ceiling.

The baseline scenario, therefore, assumes that a slightly less 1¾ percent yearly growth rate in per worker production can be realized in the coming half century.
Note that ongoing research in so-called endogenous growth models suggests that the aging of the working population may induce incentives to invest in human capital, which, in turn, would increase economic growth in the long run[1]. Though the assumption of 1¾ percent productivity growth is not excessive, appropriate policy measures should be taken in respect of labour supply, investment in human capital and technology to ensure that it will be realized. Of crucial importance is whether economic and fiscal policy measures to further increase the female labour force participation, that of people over 55 years of age and of allochthones – and particularly to reduce the persistently high disability rates e.g. in the Netherlands – are successful.

Less optimistic scenarios

Present day economic outlook gives rise to various less optimistic scenarios. The first one assumes – maintaining 1¾ percent productivity growth in the first two decades – after 2020 a yearly growth rate of 1 percent in the EU-15, Northern America and Japan. Findings are shown in Table *B1*.
Secondly, more recent studies indicate lower productivity rates also over the first 20 years of the current century. L.J. Kotlikoff et al. [2001] for the US and the EU Economic Policy Committee in its 'Lisbon scenario' [2000]) for the EU-15 assume a productivity growth over the first half of the current century of only 1 percent annually. Findings are shown in Table *B2*.
Thirdly, a worst-case scenario characterized by negative 1 percent growth in the first decade, zero growth in the second decade and a slight recovery of 1 percent growth only over the three decades after 2020 is shown in Table *B3*.

Table B1. **Less optimistic scenario: welfare in western countries and Japan in the years 2020 and 2050 (indexes[1]), the year 2000: 100), assuming 1¾ percent yearly production growth till 2020 and 1 percent after 2020; some increase in the labour force participation rate under an aging population and an unchanged (non-aging) population**

Year	2020		2050	
	Aging	Non-aging	Aging	Non-aging
Country				
(1)	(2)	(3)	(4)	(5)
EU-15	**144.7**	**151.0**	**169.2**	**203.5**
Belgium	146.7	152.3	176.6	205.4
France	142.8	148.7	175.5	200.4
Germany	138.8	146.5	165.4	197.5
Italy	147.7	155.6	158.8	209.6
Netherlands	141.7	151.1	172.8	203.6
Spain	149.2	153.5	153.3	206.9
Sweden	133.8	142.0	170.6	191.4
UK	139.9	143.2	169.8	193.0
Other world				
US	133.1	133.9	167.5	187.2
Japan	120.4	138.4	143.3	186.6
Canada	135.2	141.2	164.3	190.4

Table B2. **Less optimistic scenario: welfare in western countries and Japan in the years 2020 and 2050 (indexes[1], the year 2000: 100), assuming 1 percent yearly production growth over the whole period; some increase in the labour force participation rate under an aging population and an unchanged (non-aging) population**

Year	2020		2050	
	Aging	Non-aging	Aging	Non-aging
Country				
(1)	(2)	(3)	(4)	(5)
EU-15	**124.8**	**130.2**	**145.9**	**175.5**
Belgium	126.5	131.3	152.3	177.0
France	123.2	128.2	151.4	172.8
Germany	119.8	126.4	142.2	170.3
Italy	127.4	134.2	137.0	180.9
Netherlands	122.2	130.3	148.5	175.6
Spain	128.7	132.4	132.2	178.4
Sweden	117.3	122.4	147.1	165.0
UK	120.7	123.5	146.5	166.4
Other world				
US	114.7	119.8	144.4	161.4
Japan	103.9	119.4	123.6	160.9
Canada	116.6	121.8	141.7	164.2

Table B3. **Worst case scenario: welfare in western countries and Japan in the years 2020 and 2050 (indexes[1)], the year 2000: 100), assuming -1 percent yearly production growth till 2010, 0 percent production growth in the decade 2010-2020 and 1 percent growth over the period 2020-2050; some increase in the labour force participation rate under an aging population and an unchanged (non-aging) population**

Year	2020		2050	
	Aging	Non-aging	Aging	Non-aging
Country				
(1)	(2)	(3)	(4)	(5)
EU-15	**92.6**	**96.6**	**108.3**	**130.2**
Belgium	93.9	97.4	113.0	131.3
France	91.4	95.1	112.3	128.2
Germany	88.8	93.8	105.5	126.4
Italy	94.6	99.6	101.6	134.2
Netherlands	90.7	96.7	110.2	130.3
Spain	95.5	98.2	98.1	132.4
Sweden	87.0	90.8	109.2	122.4
UK	89.5	91.6	108.7	123.5
Other world				
US	85.1	88.9	107.2	119.8
Japan	77.1	88.6	91.7	119.4
Canada	86.5	90.4	105.2	121.8

Table B4. (More, normal and less) happy countries: welfare in Eastern European and less developed countries in the years 2020 and 2050 (indexes[1], the year 2000: 100), assuming different yearly production growth rates; a slight increase in the labour force participation rate under an aging population

Year Country (1)	2020 (2)	2050 (3)
More happy countries (3½ percent annual growth; year 2000: 100)		
Poland	209.5	493.2
Czech Republic	184.3	419.1
Romania	209.3	487.2
Hungary	220.5	521.1
China	212.3	515.5
India	227.8	610.1
Happy countries (2½ percent annual growth; year 2000: 100)		
Pakistan	204.2	431.7
Indonesia	181.6	351.1
Iran	205.4	382.6
Turkey	187.6	340.3
Brazil	182.4	340.3
Mexico	188.1	359.5
Argentina	177.4	354.1
Less happy countries (zero growth; year 2000: 100)		
Russia	104.7	92.8
Ukraine	105.6	92.8
Egypt	116.6	110.8
Nigeria	112.0	127.2
Kenya	129.3	131.7
South Africa	108.8	112.1

Finally, in the foregoing Table *B4* the welfare growth of more happy countries (3½ percent annual growth rate), (normal) happy countries (2½ percent annual growth rate) and less happy countries (zero growth) is shown.

Appendix C. Relative merits of pay-as-you-go and funding systems

There are at least two main reasons why pay-as-you-go programs have proven to be so popular in the decades following the Second World War. First, in a funded system it will take many years to build up a reasonable pension. In contrast, under a pay-as-you-go system a full pension can be paid immediately, with a transitional gain to retirees and the older cohorts of workers. Starting a pay-as-you-go scheme – mostly covering the national territory – in the years following the Second World War was rather easy, as the ratio of workers to pensioners and the expected population trends were favourable. There have been some definite winners and no losers or, in other words, when the pay-as-you-go schemes were installed, the first generation(s) of pensioners had a 'free lunch'; they received pensions without or only partially having contributed[2]. Secondly, because pensions are paid out of workers' contributions, they can be increased – reflecting changes in prices and/or wage-level – rather easily without levying increasing contribution rates from workers' income.

C1 Guarantees and preferences

Pay-as-you-go schemes probably will be preferred in a world with large economic change and uncertainty (at least when a continuing flow of contributions in a designated geographical area can be relied upon). Of particular relevance is that pay-as-you-go systems stand the risk of a low real rate of investment return and low asset prices due to persistent (and unexpected) inflation, a high capital intensity and other unforeseen events over which society has no control. Under a pay-as-you-go based system society – though it can definitely not guarantee a previously promised level of pensions – can better control the conditions of the social contract between generations. On the other hand the aging linked perpetual rise in pay-as-you-go contribution rates may contribute to higher labour costs and labour market distortions, hence a higher future unemployment level and a smaller coverage, thereby deteriorating the conditions of long-term viability.
Furthermore, pay-as-you-go schemes are said to minimize impediments to labour mobility at home, but generally not across national borders.

Undoubtedly one of the most important features of a funded occupational plan is that its premium payments are less likely to be regarded as taxes.

---

2 On the other hand, when transforming a pay-as-you-go plan to a funded scheme, the 'last generation' of workers will pay twice: for the present pensioners and for their own funded scheme. There appear to be definite losers and no winners, so the argument goes. But it is not so dramatic as that, as workers acquire in turn the ownership of capital assets and lower consumption today – or increased own saving – is balanced by greater resources for consumption in the future. The path from pay-as-you-go to fully funded schemes nevertheless will always be rather long.

rather than as own savings for an old-age provision (less difference between gross and net wage level), thereby avoiding to a large extent negative labour market distortions and probably giving rise to increased labour force participation[3]. Clearly, this is beneficial for the economy as a whole, especially in countries where companies and workers are heavily engaged in the informal sector. In Latin-American countries e.g. half of the labour force or more is in the informal sector (IBRD [1994]). Generally, a large informal sector diminishes the financial capacity of a basic old-age pension system based on pay-as-you-go; it also hurts the government's fiscal capacity, thereby crowding-out the supply of other important categories of public goods as well. In the worst case evasion can lead to the (near) collapse of the pension system, particularly when workers evade contributions but still qualify for benefits.
In a politically turbulent/destabilized world with insufficient self-control serious problems will arise in maintaining pay-as-you-go systems. Personal defined contribution plans may then be the only attractive or feasible alternative.

Funding can make another psychological difference as there is anticipatory behaviour involved and this may be one of the advantages of funding. The major advantage in our view is the ownership of capital. A major disadvantage of the funding principle remains that inflation has to be considered as an uninsurable risk, as it affects everyone.
For an individual contribution paying person a pay-as-you-go plan is preferential to funding when the sum of the rates of growth of population (n) and of real wages (g) exceeds the rate of interest (r). This is termed the Aaron-condition or Aaron-rule, which rule is well known. The returns from both pension finance systems to the contribution payer are identical when $r = g + n$. It appears that what is true on a micro-level is not necessarily (always) true on a macro-level.
Today pay-as-you-go plans have lost much of their popularity in many countries, being accused of costing too much and having an adverse impact on the economy in an aging society. Funded schemes have received much more emphasis in the last few decades as a result of changing concepts about (personal) responsibilities and choices and more fiscal incentives to provide for one's own pension income. Remember however the warning of N. Barr against '... reliance on funding *alone* to address demographic problems [...]. To imagine that funded schemes are substantially better in the face of aggregate uncertainty is to fall for crude mythology.'

3 It can be doubted, however, whether premium payments are considered as own savings rather than taxes when the funded (supplementary) pension system is organized on a collective basis, which happens to be the case in The Netherlands. Otherwise, an individual's pension can be closely linked to contributions paid during his working years under a pay-as-you-go system as well (system of notional funding).

C2 Labour supply and savings

Next, there is the aspect of international competitiveness of jobs. Consider two countries identical in all respects but towards the financing of their pension scheme: one is more relying on pay-as-you-go than the other. When borders are open to labour migration of the young, one can expect an outflow from the 'more indebted' country to the 'less indebted' country. If, furthermore, the population is aging there is an additional incentive for the young generation to move out from the pay-as-you-go country to a funded country due to high labour costs, high taxes and lower net income. As a consequence, countries dedicated to the pay-a-you-go principle and resisting even a partial shift towards funded schemes can be forced to reform the finance, because of mobility-induced tax competition[4].

Evidently a major difference between funding and pay-as-you-go is that funding is generally leading to an additional flow of saving during the period of growing up – and under circumstances also in an aging economy with economic growth –, thereby creating a resource base, which enables higher levels of production and consumption for both future workers and retirees. From a theoretical point of view the condition of optimal savings has to be fulfilled. If savings accumulated to provide for an old-age pension income, together with all other sources of saving, would yield over-accumulation, the pay-as-you-go share in pension financing should be increased in order to attain what economists call the 'golden rule'-level. Similarly, if in the steady-state equilibrium stage, the economy would be undercapitalised, public and private pension arrangements should rely more heavily on funding. The test for this latter condition is that the total return to capital exceeds the sum of growth of population and output per worker.

C3 Conditions to be fulfilled

The idea of stimulating economic growth by building up a larger capital stock by pension saving is based on four major assumptions.

First, additional pension saving increases, at least in part, total national saving, as long as there are no offsetting reactions by households, firms or government. For instance, savings within a public fund may be offset by increased spending in other government programs, leading to disserving to a certain extent and reduced savings in other forms might offset savings within private complementary schemes. If pension savings simply replace other savings, it makes little real difference. Saving rates in countries like the United Kingdom and the Netherlands with high pension assets are rather similar to that in Germany (W. Schmaltz [1998]).

Secondly, the savings will lead to investments that increase the capital formation and the productive capacity of a country. Or, in other words, investments do not fall short of the savings level. But this is not an automatic process; economies do not behave like well-oiled equilibrium machines. If savings fall behind, this can result in increased hoardings and decreased national income levels (the Keynesian

4 A. Jousten and P. Pestieau [2001].

model) or in a (larger) surplus on the current account of the balance of payments (the neo-classical model). If pension savings lead to new productive investments – which would not otherwise have occurred – then funding can make a real difference. The second condition unfortunately was not or at best only partially fulfilled in e.g. The Netherlands during the last few decades, where investments fell behind national savings, leading to a large surplus on the current account of the balance of payments. Note that for a small open economy assets abroad can be beneficial[5].

Third, the capital stock is smaller than according to the 'golden rule'-level or, in other words, national savings are below their optimal level and are expected to persist for a long time period ahead.

Fourth, increased pension saving must be the best way to stimulate productivity. If increasing the national saving rate were a main reason to fund pension plans, there could be found other and maybe even better ways to accomplish this goal[6]. The government, for example could run a surplus on its budget, thereby creating government savings or use various kinds of incentives stimulating private savings. If there is an alternative policy to promote savings and productivity either more efficiently or with less risk, then it might be the preferred policy. Other fiscal policy measures may provide the government with more direct means of stimulating both public and private saving, thereby avoiding increasing public deficits – and possibly also a lower aggregate savings ratio – due to a smaller amount of tax receipts[7].

---

5 A large amount of foreign assets enables a country to maintain the consumption of the population with goods produced abroad. It has to be pointed out that major difficulties will arise on the meso and micro level, as foreign accounts are to a large extent owned by companies and banks and not by individuals or organizations of individuals. Thus, (Dutch) pension funds should invest on a wider scale abroad, e.g. in the newly industrialized economies.

6 Pension savings might be unstable in some way or other. In a steady state economy with a stable age distribution of the population and with zero income growth, saving by the working population exactly balances dissaving by the retired. Aggregate net savings are zero, as with a pay-as-you-go based pension system. Thus, at first sight there is no real difference between both pension finance systems. In an equilibrium stage a funded system does not make a (major) contribution to the growth of the capital stock. In an aging population aggregate pension saving will be negative and in a growing population – a period during which pension funds are building up – pension savings are positive. Funding may be preferential and more favorable nevertheless. In the built-up phase to steady state the aggregate saving ratio and capital formation are increased. After several decades the increased dissaving among retirees will approximately offset the amount of savings of the younger population and the aggregate saving ratio will return to its previous lower level. The capital stock however is larger and thereby the production per worker. Or, in other words, the economy has settled to a new steady state with a higher level of income and production.
For the US S.J. Schieber and J.B. Shoven [1997] show findings from scenario-analyses, '... the pension system would continue to generate significant investable funds for the next 20 years or so. By 2024 the pension system is projected to cease being a net source of saving for the economy and in fact to become from that point increasingly a net dissaver.'

7 Ideally the contribution level should reflect the liabilities that are being incurred and send the correct and timely signals. This is definitely not a characteristic of the pay-as-you-go system, but such a missing link can be established also without building up a fund. The government

C4 Does funding matter?

When the four conditions referred to are fulfilled, the question whether funding matters and could be part of the solution to the problems caused by e.g. adverse demographic developments (and deteriorating ecological conditions) can be answered in the affirmative[8]. A higher degree of funding in financing the national pension system will enhance national welfare. Funding will be preferential to the extent that it causes national product to be higher. It will be clear that the costs of population aging cannot be avoided. On the other hand by increasing investments now – the economic costs of it or the benefits forgone are the reduced current consumption expenditures of the present generations – one is anticipating the difficulties that could otherwise (with no-funding) arise in an economy with a lower national product. This favours future generations.

A further expansion of funded occupational supplementary pension plans can be considered as an adequate, but not a unique mechanism to promote savings.

Note however that pension finance systems are not created, at least not in the first place, because of the impact they might have on the performance of the national economy. Foremost, they are designed as mechanisms to adequately provide for pension incomes to the elderly. On the other hand, the two purposes do not necessarily exclude each other, they can be compatible.

Apart from the impact funding can have on the size of future productive capacity, pension saving might be particularly preferential to people as more security can be obtained compared with pay-as-you-go. Or, in other words, the major (economic) difference between funding and pay-as-you-go goes beyond the macro-economic issues of savings and investment.

---

can levy higher taxes or contributions thereby reducing borrowing and diminishing the size of public debt. Decreasing interest payments on public debt can compensate future increases in contribution rates of pay-as-you-go pension plans. This principle (of *notional funding*) underlies the financing practice in respect of the basic pension scheme (AOW) in the Netherlands. From a fiscal point of view the policy of reducing the public debt/GNP ratio (in advance of coming demographic pressure) is 'equivalent' to accumulating a fund.

8 Note that on the micro-level decisions in respect of financing pensions are taken with a view to interests of employers and employees only. Pension schemes should be and actually are an instrument for providing old-age pensions, not for increasing the volume of national savings (nor for improving the functioning of financial markets or for being an instrument for labour market policy). Thus, the national concern (achieving the optimal savings level) and participants' interest (providing for adequate old-age pension provisions) do not automatically match; generally speaking they do not. These interests may be reconciled by well-chosen economic and fiscal policy measures, e.g. adequate tax treatment. Countervailing policy measures of the government in respect of savings might be necessary.

References

Barr, N. (2002): Reforming pensions: Myths, truths, and policy choices. International Social Security Review 55, 3-36

Jousten, A., Pestieau, P. (2001): Labor mobility, redistribution and pension reform in Europe, In: Feldstein, M., Siebert, H. (eds.): Social security pension reforms in Europe. Conference proceedings, University of Chicago Press, Chicago, 85-108.

Orszag, P.R., Stiglitz, J.E. (2001): Rethinking pension reform: ten myths about social security. In: Holzmann, R., Stiglitz, J.E. (eds.): New ideas about old age security. The World Bank, Washington, D.C.

Schieber, S.J., Shoven, J.B. (1997): The consequences of population aging on private pension fund saving and asset markets. In: Schieber, S.J., Shoven, J.B. (eds.): Public policies towards pensions. MIT Press, Cambridge, MA, 219-246.

Schmähl, W. (1998): Comment on .... In: Siebert, H. (ed.): Redesigning social security. Mohr Siebeck, Tübingen, 186-196.

Appendix D. Neo-classical economics in a growing older environment

The three conditions of equilibrium in the neo-classical approach are full capacity, full employment and equality of savings and investments. We consider a production function of the Cobb-Douglas form, with Harrod-neutral technical progress at rate m and with constant returns to scale,

$$Y(t) = K^{\mu}(t).\bar{L}^{1-\mu}(t) \tag{1}$$

All variables are taken as continuous and differentiable functions of time. Y is total output per unit of time, K is capital stock and $\bar{L}$ is labour supply measured in efficiency units at any point of time: $\bar{L}(t) = L(t).e^{mt}$ and $L(t) = L(0).e^{nt}$, where n is the (working) population growth rate. Moreover investments equal savings: $DK(t) = sY(t)$ where s is the savings ratio. Assume $m = 0$ for expositional ease. The exponents μ and $1-\mu$ are constants representing the relative share of capital and labour in national product.

In per workers terms and deleting the time-index equation (1) reduces to,

$$y = f(k) = k^{\mu} \tag{2}$$

where $y = Y/L$ and $k = K/L$.

The marginal products (of capital and labour) are,

$$\partial Y/\partial K = f'(k) = \mu.k^{\mu-1} \tag{3}$$

$$\partial Y/\partial L = y - f'(k).k = (1-\mu).k^{\mu} \tag{4}$$

When production is based on profit maximisation under perfect competition on both product and input markets, the profit rate (r) and the wage rate (w) are equal to their marginal products. A production function with constant returns to scale guarantees that the payment of marginal products to the factors of production will exactly exhaust total production,

$$Y = K.\partial Y/\partial K + L.\partial Y/\partial L \tag{5}$$

D.1 The golden rule growth path

Maintaining constant capital intensity[9] the required investments per worker are nk and, hence, production per worker available for consumption (c) is,

$$c = f(k) - nk \tag{6}$$

The condition for optimal per capita consumption ('golden rule growth path') follows from,

$$\partial c/\partial k = f'(k) - n = 0 \tag{7}$$

yielding $r = n$, i.e. the interest or profit rate equals the population growth rate.

D.2 Marginal product of capital

Introducing depreciation of capital at rate h, it follows from $d\log Y/d\log K = (K/Y)/(dY/dK)$, $dK = sY - cK$ and $Y/K = (g+h)/s$ that,

$$\partial Y/\partial K = \mu.(Y/K) = \mu.((g+h)/s), \tag{8}$$

with $g = m+n$ and m is not necessarily zero; the marginal product of capital is denoted by 'mpc' for short.

Hence, the change in the marginal product of capital from a slowdown in the labour force growth is,

$$d(mpc)/dn = \mu/s, \tag{9}$$

Similarly, we can consider the effect of a change in the savings rate and in the rate of technical progress on the marginal product of capital,

$$d(mpc)/ds = -\mu.((g+h)/s^2), \tag{10}$$

$$d(mpc)/dm = \mu/s \tag{11}$$

Clearly,

$$d(mpc)/dg = \mu/s \tag{12}$$

Note that these effects are attenuated to the extent that the economy is open.

---

9 Maintaining capital intensity is obtained when $k = (s/n).(1/(1-\mu))$, where s is the saving rate out of national product. The theory of neo-classical growth models can be found in every macroeconomic textbook.

D.3 Neo-classical economics and the overlapping generations approach

Neo-classical economics and the overlapping generations approach can be synthesized by decomposing the consumption level in equation (6) into the consumption of two successive generations. Denote actual per capita consumption of the working population as c^{worker} and that of the retired population as $c^{retired}$, assuming away the non-working age group of say 0-19 years of age. In any period of time the number of the working population is (1+n) times the size of the retired population, being the working population in the former period. It can be shown that,

$$c^{retired} / (1+n) + c^{worker} = f(k) - nk \qquad (13)$$

The left-hand side of equation (13) represents the optimal life-cycle allocation of consumption by individuals, that is realized for $r=n$ (Samuelson [1958, 1975[a,b]])[10]. The right-hand side represents the (optimal) allocation of production capacity to consumption goods, given necessary investments (nk) to maintain the capital-labour ratio.
Savings must equal investments and be just sufficient as well to satisfy individual life-cycle plans. The required interest rate (r^*) to guarantee desired consumption during old age and optimal allocation of production as well follows from (14) below and equals the population growth rate (n) under golden rule growth conditions,

$$f(k) - r^*.k - c^{worker} = c^{retired} / (1+r^*) = k.(1+r^*) \qquad (14)$$

When there is oversaving or undersaving in the economy, leading to a per worker capital stock that is too high or too low respectively, the existence (and the introduction) of an old-age pension system may provide a mechanism to deal with the disequilibrium problem by allowing the possibility of underfunding and overfunding in financing the pension plan.

D.4 Consumption and demographic change

Actual per capita (of the total population) consumption is only a part (p) of the output net of investment per worker. This part is the ratio of the number of workers to the size of the population, also termed the dependency ratio. Hence, per capita consumption ($c^{tot.\ pop.}$) follows from (6),

---

10 With no time preference and assuming no technical progress (g=0), the Samuelson *consumption loan* model specified that r=n solved the problem of life-cycle consumption allocation (and of the within-period equilibrium in respect of net savings of the generations living in any period). This result can be extended to positive productivity growth (H.J. Aaron [1966]) and also to positive time preference (O.J. Blanchard and S. Fischer [1989]).

$$c^{tot.\ pop.} = p.\{\ f(k)\ -\ nk\ \} \tag{15}$$

Equation (10) can be rewritten to find the change in $c^{tot.\ pop.}$ $(= c^{t.p.})$ in response to changes of the population growth rate (n) and of the dependency ratio (p),

$$(\Delta c^{t.p.})/c^{t.p.} = (\Delta p)/p - \Delta n.\{p.(k/c^{t.p.}) + \Delta p.(k/c^{t.p.})\} \tag{16}$$

with c, k and p evaluated at the initial steady state. It is also assumed that the capital-labour ratio is unaffected by a demographic change.

A decline in the dependency ratio (Δp is negative) reduces the level of per capita consumption that is feasible given the economy's capital stock. In contrast, a decline in the growth rate of the working population (Δn is negative) leads to a rise of the per capita consumption level given the value of the capital intensity (k). The latter effect, also termed the 'Solow-effect', permits society to consume more ('the consumption dividend'), while it is able to invest less and still maintain the per worker production level[11].
In the short run the Solow-effect probably offsets the long-run dependency effect and, hence, the consumption level increases. In the long run the sustainable consumption level will decline as the dependency increases.
The effect on consumption of a demographic shift such as fertility decline, which reduces both p and n, depends on which of these effects is the larger.

References

Aaron, H.J. (1966): The social insurance paradox. Canadian Journal of Economic and Political Science 32, 371-74.

Blanchard, O.J., Fischer, S. (1989): Lectures on Macroeconomics. MIT Press, Cambridge, MA.

Cutler, D.M., Poterba, J.M., Sheiner, L.M., Summers, L.H. (1990): An aging society: opportunity or challenge? Brookings Papers on Economic Activity 1, 1990, 1-73.

---

11 Under golden rule growth conditions (cf. equation (7)), $\partial c/\partial n = -k$. Reductions in n reduce the steady state saving rate. This is easily seen from the Harrod-Domar condition for steady-state growth that the capital-output ratio is constant: $f(k)/k = n/s =$ constant. Hence, per capita consumption can increase.

Diamond, P.A. (2000): What stock market returns to expect for the future. Social Security Bulletin 63, 38-48.

Disney, R. (1996): Can we afford to grow older? MIT Press, Cambridge, MA.

Samuelson, P.A. (1958): An exact consumption-loan model of interest with or without the social contrivance of money. Journal of Political Economy 66, 467-482

Samuelson, P.A. (1975[a]): The optimum growth rate for population. International Economic Review 16, 531-538.

Samuelson, P.A. (1975[b]): Optimum social security in a life-cycle growth model. International Economic Review 16, 539-544.

Appendix E. Aging in the Netherlands

Also in the Netherlands aging will be one of the major policy issues in the coming decades. This Appendix heavily draws on a study of CPB Netherlands Bureau for Economic Policy Analysis, *Ageing in the Netherlands*, published in 2000. The main focus of the CPB-study is on the sustainability of public finance.

E1 Assumptions and main developments

E1.1 Demography

Total population of the Netherlands – projection-2001 of *CBS Statistics Netherlands (SN)* – grows from 15.9 million in 2000 to 17.5 million in 2020 and a slightly less 18.0 million by 2050. The latest projection (SN2001) differs from the projection-1998 (SN1998), as shown in table E1. Declining fertility rates and increasing life expectancy contributed to the aging of the population in the last three decades. Aging will considerably change the age distribution in the coming decades. The well-known dependency ratio – population aged 65 and over divided by population aged 20 to 64 – increases from 0.22 in 2000 to a peak level of 0.42 by 2040. After 2050 the share of older people will remain high, stabilizing on a level around 0.40.
The demographic transition will have significant consequences for the government budget and for social security outlays, and may lead to increasing deficits and increasing public debt if no adequate fiscal policy measures are taken.

Table E1. Population of the Netherlands (2000-2050)

Age distribution	2000	2020		2050	
		SN1998	SN2001	SN1998	SN2001
0-19	0.24	0.22	0.23	0.22	0.23
20-64	0.62	0.59	0.59	0.54	0.55
20-59	0.57	0,52	0.52	0.49	0.50
60-64	0.05	0.06	0.06	0.05	0.06
65+	0.14	0.19	0.18	0.24	0.22
dependency ratio	0.22	0.32	0.31	0.44	0.40
total (million)	15.9	17.1	17.5	17.4	18.0

E1.2 Economy

Labour productivity is assumed to increase at a yearly rate of 1.75 percent. Labour force participation is expected to grow by about 5 to 7 percentage points from 71 percent in 2000 to 77 percent in 2020 and 78 percent by 2050. The main determining factor of this increase is the rise in the female participation rate. Aging exerts a negative influence on the overall participation as older people work less than younger people. Measured in full-time equivalents the rise is markedly less with 1.5 percentage points in 2020 and 2 percentage points by 2050 since women increasingly work in part-time jobs. No account is taken of a further increase of the part of ethnic minorities in total population after 2020. As labour force participation of many ethnic groups is relatively low, this has a negative influence on the overall participation rate.

The number of people receiving disability benefits is expected to grow from 0.95 million in 2000 to 1.25 million by 2020 and following years, despite a variety of policy measures to reduce the incidence of disability. About a quarter of the increase can be explained by the aging of the working population. Half of the rise is due to the employment growth of women and the last quarter is brought about by the 'young disabled' -scheme. The use of early retirement plans will grow by 45 percent in the period 2000 to 2020 (and beyond) from 190 thousand to 250 thousand.

The capital market interest rate (risk-free assets) is assumed to be constant over time, 4 percent in real terms. Returns on equity are 8.5 percent, implying a rather high equity premium of 4.5 percent; the rate of inflation amounts to 2 percent. The rate of return on pension capital is 5¾ percent and the actual rate of wage growth (in real terms) is 1¾ percent, resulting in a real interest rate and discounting factor of 4 percent. Note that capital market returns are even more important in the Netherlands than in most other Western countries due to i.a. the large scale of the supplementary pension system. CPB's assumption of 5¾ percent return on pension capital is rather optimistic. It can be argued that long-term returns for pension funds are more likely to be 3¾ percent instead of 5¾ percent[12]. Were return on pension capital to remain around 3½ to 4 percent, contribution rates will rise considerably from 6.8 percent of total wages to 15 percent or more.

E1.3 The Dutch pension system

The pension system in the Netherlands is built up on the three pillars concept. The first pillar being public pensions, pay-as-you-go based, flat-rate and not dependent on labour history, contributions paid, wealth or other income. The second pillar consists of industry-wide and company-based mandatory pension plans, based on funding and predominantly of the defined benefit type. The third pillar is

12 Cf. David Carey [OECD, 2002]. Using the Gordon formula and growth projections for the coming half century, returns on equities seem to amount to 4 to 4½ percent and long-term government bonds are yielding 3½ percent.

comprised of individual supplementary pensions of the defined contribution type. The first pillar accounts for 40 percent of old-age income, the second pillar accounts for 50 percent and the third pillar for the remaining 10 percent. Less then 1 percent of those of age 65 and over is still working (the fourth pillar).

Table E2 shows the development of public pensions as a percentage of GDP, a moderate increase over half a century from 4.7 percent GDP to 8.5 percent by 2050 (peak level in 2040: 9 percent GDP)[13]. Complementary pension expenditures rise sharply in he coming decades from 4.1 percent GDP in 2000 to 13.1 percent by 2050. The increase in the contribution rate is modest and not before 2020; mainly due to a further rise in life expectancy the average contribution rate raises by 0.8 percentage points of wages. The pension result (the ratio of average total pension income and average final wage income) increases considerably. The complementary pension system is of increasing importance in providing for old-age income; its share in total income of the elderly rises with about 10 percentage points. Figures for the year 2050 are interpolated.
Higher participation also results in a steady increase of pension fund assets. Clearly there are no pension dissavings in the first half of the 21st century and beyond.

Table E2. Pension aggregates (2000-2050)

	2001	2020	2050
public pensions (% GDP)	4.7	6,8	8.5
complementary pensions			
expenditures (% GDP)	4.1	7.3	13.1
contributions (% wages)	6.8	6.8	7.6
pension result (% final income)	38.1	42.4	52.1
pension assets (% GDP)	121	172	187

The ratio of health care expenditures to GDP rises from 7.0 percent in 2000 to 10.5 percent in 2050.

13 According to Sociale Verzekeringsbank (Social Insurance Institution [2001]) basic pension expenditures in 2040 amount to 7 percent GDP and in 2050 about 6.5 percent, opposed to CPB with 9 and 8,5 percent respectively (year 2050 my interpolation).

E1.4 Public finance

Public expenditures as a percentage of GDP will rise from 44.9 in 2000 to 54.4 in 2050. Revenues will grow from 45.8 percent GDP in 2000 to 50 percent by 2050, giving rise to a deficit of 4.4 percent GDP. Sustainability of public finances is achieved by raising indirect taxes in 2001 by 0.7 percentage points of GDP. This is relatively mild increase of the national tax burden. As a result government debt (EMU definition) decreases from 54 percent GDP in 2000 to about 10 percent in 2050. Due to considerably lower interest payments public expenditures now grow to over 50,5 percent of GDP in 2050, a difference of 4.9 percentage points compared with the budget without policy adjustment. Revenues exceed or are roughly equal to expenditures over the period until 2050, leading to a surplus and a balanced budget respectively. Income tax from pension income rises from 1.8 percent GDP in 2001 to 4.9 percent in 2050.
We may conclude therefore that thanks to the reversal in the tax expenditures of private pension plans and to the shrinking government debt from 54 percent in 2001 to about 10 percent by 2050, fiscal room is created to meet the additional expenditures in health care and public pensions. This is rather unique to the Netherlands compared with most other aging countries.
Note however that diminishing public debt per se does not increase the productive capacity of the economy.

If higher taxes have a negative impact on economic activity in the long run – through the impact of the tax wedge on employment and production – the indirect tax rate should be raised by 1.0 percent GDP.
A worst-case scenario, characterized by one year higher life expectancy and no increase in the labour force participation gives rise to an unsustainability of public finance. In 2040 the budget deficit (EMU definition) amounts to 8.9 percent GDP and government debt is 120 percent GDP. Sustainability can be achieved by an adjustment of indirect tax rates of 2.1 percentage points (rather than 0.7 points).

E1.5 Economic aggregates in the long term[14]

Table E3 shows the major economic aggregates projected for the period ahead, from 2000 to 2050 in a scenario with sustainable public finances. It appears that the coming demographic transition leads to considerable increase in consumption relative to domestic production (GDP). Domestic production grows by a steady-state rate, equal to the growth rate of the employed working population and the productivity growth. Hence, in the coming two decades GDP yearly grows by close to 2 percent; in the period 2020-2050 by about 1½ percent annually.

---

14 Using CPB's lower labour force participation rates and slightly different demographic data our simplified analysis yields an increase of the production of consumptional goods and services (being a constant share of GDP) from 100 in 2000 to 150 in 2020 and 237 in 2050, almost equal to CPB's findings of GDP: 147 in 2020 and 233 in 2050 (2000 =100).

In contrast, D.P. Broer [2001] is less optimistic on growth rates of the economy. Scarcity of labour – the participation rate slightly falls until 2030 – has an adverse effect on investment and output growth. On the transition path the actual growth rate is half a percent below the steady-state rate (2 percent annually) over the next three decades. The accumulated decline in per capita output results in an output loss of 12 percent as compared with the steady-state path.

A rising share of pension income pushes private consumption from its current level of 50 percent GDP to 59 percent. Government consumption increases from 23 percent to 27 percent GDP over the first half of the 21st century. Investment expenditures are rather constant with 20 percent GDP. As a result domestic spending grows at a higher rate than domestic production and, hence, the trade balance that today shows a surplus of 5 percent will turn into a deficit of 6 percent in 2050.

Table E3. Economic aggregates (percentages GDP; 2000-2050)

	2000	**2020**	**2050**
GDP (2000 = 100)	100	147	233
average annual growth (%)	2	1.5	1.8
spending (GDP = 100)			
private consumption	50	54	59
government consumption	23	24	26
investments	23	20	20
	—	—	—
domestic spending	95	98	106
trade balance (GDP = 100)	5	2	-6
net income from foreign assets	1	7	10
balance of payments	6	8	4
GNP (GDP=100)	101	107	110
net foreign assets (GDP=100)	2	97	230

The large trade surpluses during many years induce capital export of equal size, leading to a significant accumulation of foreign assets. This financial asset position generates in turn net capital income of 7 percent GDP in 2020 and 10 percent in 2050. Net foreign assets amount to 97 percent GDP in 2020 and about 230 percent by 2050, a tremendous increase compared with the tiny start position of 2 percent today. Capital income from abroad, hence, can more than compensate the trade balance deficit. As a result the balance of payments still shows a surplus. There is room for a further growth of consumption relative to production.

Note that not all aging countries can follow a policy of foreign assets accumulation, as the global balance of payment sum is zero.

E2 Consumption and welfare

In our previous analysis it is also assumed that 1¾ percent yearly growth rate in per worker production can be realized in the coming decades and that the labour force participation ratio in the Netherlands increases from 0.71 in 2000 to 0.77 in 2020, more than in the CPB-analysis. We use (more recent) CBS demographic data of 2001 opposed to CPB, which uses CBS data-1998.
In 2000 the per capita consumption of persons aged 20-64 is 100, that of young ones (mostly children) 50 and that the consumption level of older people is still lagging behind somewhat at 80 (Table E4). Hence, total consumption in the baseline year is 8508 (index).
Per capita consumption is a measure of personal welfare. Total consumption expenditures are a stable share of total national output. Under these assumptions the proportion of gross domestic product (GDP) allocated for personal consumption expenditures in 2020 amounts to 13814, which enables an average per capita consumption of 141.8 for all people over 20 years of age. Note that in 2020 equal consumption opportunities exist for the active population and the elderly. The end of the struggle for emancipation.
Consumption of the working age population increases in the period 2000 to 2020 by 41.8 percent and that of the 65^+-population by 77 percent (from index 80 to index 141.8).
In an unchanged population (no aging from 2000 onwards) per capita consumption would be 151.1 for all people over 20 years of age instead of 141.8. The difference between the indexes 151.1 and 141.8 can be considered as the consumption sacrifice or the volume of consumptional expenditures forgone by the younger population groups in favour of the elderly.
Between 2020 and 2050 per capita consumption according to rather optimistic assumptions in respect of labour force participation and productivity growth increase with 1.6 percent annually from index 141.8 to index 225.9.

Table E4. Production and welfare in the Netherlands in the years 2000, 2020 and 2050 (indexes[1]) for different population cohorts, 0-19y, 20-64y and 65+ years of age, assuming 1¾ percent yearly production growth and a labour force participation rate of 0.77 by 2020 and beyond opposed to 0.71 in 2000 (demographic projection SN2001)

Age	Population	Working-population	C/population	Y/working-population	C(=Y)
(1)	(2)	(3)	(4)	(5)	(6)
2000 (*present time*)					
0-19	24.4	-	50	-	1220
20-64	62.0	44.0	100	193,2	6201
65+	13.6	-	80	-	1087
total	**100.0**	**44.0**	ave. **85.1**	total **8508**	**8508**
2020 (medium term)					
0-19	25.2	-	70.9	-	1787
20-64	64.6	49.7	141.8	277.8	9156
65+	20.3	-	141.8	-	2871
total	**110.1**	**49.7**	ave. **125.5**	total **13814**	**13814**
2050 (long term)					
0-19	25.8	-	112.9	-	2912
20-64	63.0	48.5	225.9	467.4	14220
65+	24.5	-	225.9	-	5526
total	**113.2**	**48.5**	ave. **200.2**	total **22658**	**22658**

1) C is consumption and Y is a part of gross domestic product

E2.1 Alternative presentations

Table E5 below shows the consumption level of the adult population in 2020 (2000 being 100) with different labour force participation rates and different growth rates of production per worker. The pessimistic –1/0 scenario consists of a sad –1 percent annual growth in the first decade and only a slightly better zero growth in 2010-2020. Per capita welfare decreases with 10 to 15 percent. The other scenarios fare better. Only with an constant or slightly increasing labour force participation rate (of 0.71 and 0.74 respectively) as in the baseline year and a zero growth rate of production per worker, the consumption level of the adult population is decreasing from 100 in 2000 to 92.4 and 96.3 respectively in 2020, which seems serious but far from dramatic. In all other scenarios, however, the standard of living can be maintained and there is still room for a further increase, ranging from a modest 112.7 to an impressive 148.9.

Table E5. Consumption level of the 20^{+}- population in 2020 (indexes) under different growth rates of production per worker and different labour force participation rates (2000: 100)

	Growth rate of production per worker (%)			
Participation rate	-1/0	0	1	2
0,71	84.4	92.4	112.7	137.3
0,74	87.1	96.3	117.5	143.1
0,77	90.6	100.2	122.3	148.9

We can also reverse the question and examine which yearly growth rate of labour productivity is necessary to offset the negative impact of population aging on living standards or average per capita consumption in 2020. The question which level of productivity growth is necessary to arrive at a 15 percent, 30 percent or 60 percent growth of average per capita consumption over the time period 2000-2020 is also answered. Evidence is presented in Table E6.

It turns out that a modest to moderate rate of technological progress is (necessary and) sufficient to offset the adverse consequences of aging on the level of consumption and welfare. With constant labour force participation rate of the working age population a growth rate of average production per worker of 0.4 percent suffices[15]. The required productivity growth rate is small compared with the productivity growth in the past two decades, which amounted to about 2½ percent. Furthermore, a growth rate of production per worker of zero necessitates the labour force ratio to rise to 0.77 to offset any detrimental effect of population aging on welfare by 2020.

Table E6. Growth rate of production per worker (percentage) necessary to achieve zero percent, 15 percent, 30 percent or 60 percent higher level of consumption of the 20^{+}- population in 2020 under different labour force participation rates

	Desired growth rate of consumption level from 2000 to 2020 (%)			
Participation rate	0	15	30	60
0,71	0.4	1.1	1.7	2.8
0,74	0.2	0.9	1.5	2.6
0,77	-0.01	0.7	1.3	2.4

On the other hand, a yearly growth rate of labour productivity ranging between 1.5 percent and 2.5 percent, depending on labour force participation, give rise to satisfying welfare increases in the year 2020 vis à vis the year 2000, varying between 24 percent and 60 percent.

Under constant labour force participation the working age population in 2020 must be 16.9 percent larger relative to its size shown in Table 1A to ensure a constant per capita welfare level and in 2050 even 41 percent larger. Those increases in the size of the working-age population are realized by immigration from outside the EU-15. Research in the Netherlands has shown conclusively that the costs of immigration in the second half of the 20th century have greatly exceeded the benefits[16].

15 It can make a difference for workers' perception of bearing the pension burden in an aging population whether GDP growth is reached by productivity growth with a constant or even smaller labour force or by expanding the working population. In the former case higher gross wages and higher contribution rates will result than in the latter case with higher employment and slower productivity growth.

16 N. van Nimwegen and G. Beets [2000]

E2.2 Policy measures

With growth in the working age population slowing down to close to zero over the coming decades, further increase in welfare will predominantly depend on labour productivity growth. As pointed out in the main text to stimulate productivity growth bold comprehensive policy measures are necessary aimed at strengthening economic and social fundamentals, improving functioning of markets and above all investing more in education and training for all workers of all ages, but particularly in the human capital of the youngest generations.
Reducing the non-participation of the (pre-)elderly, women and other inactive people remains of relevance. The routes to early withdrawal from the labour force developed in the 1970's and 1980's have to be closed. Incentives not to work are removed and the pay-as-you-go based early retirement VUT-schemes are replaced by funded pre-retirement plans sooner than legislation for a phase-out of tax deductibility for VUT-schemes by 2022 allows. No accrual of pension rights during disability and unemployment as though beneficiaries were still working is recommended also.

For those reform measures to be successful, there must be jobs available for older workers and others entering the labour market. Obstacles as seniority-based pay systems and other rigidities in payment impeding labour force participation are removed. Job-related training for older workers is obligatory.

E3 Concluding observations

It can be concluded that without doubt we can afford to grow older. We in The Netherlands (and elsewhere in the developed world as well) are rich enough to sustain an old-age pension for a more numerous older population.
Aging is the result of a process of continuous and increasing civilization during the last one and half century in the developed world – first ameliorated sanitary conditions (e.g. adequate water supply, sewerage, general hygiene), furthermore a broad supply of medical services – and, hence should be applauded cheerfully and gratefully. The 'problems of aging' rather are the pessimistic way of looking at a great success of civilization.
The income and purchasing power of today's elderly are high and will be still higher tomorrow.
There is more reason to be concerned about the welfare of many younger age groups and, above all, the sustainability of an adequate health care system for the whole population as there are major bottlenecks in respect of labour supply involved. Reallocation of labour from the more productive industrial sector to the less productive sector of services will occur.
From the point of view of public finance the Netherlands are well equipped to face population aging.

References

CPB (2000): Ageing in the Netherlands, SDU, The Hague, Netherlands.

Bettendorf, L.J.H., Bovenberg, A.L., Broer, D.P. (2000): De gevolgen van vergrijzing voor de economische ontwikkeling in Nederland. OCFEB, Rotterdam.

Broer, D.P. (2001): Growth and welfare distribution in an ageing society: an applied general equilibrium analysis for the Netherlands. De Economist 149, 81-114.

Nimwegen, N., Beets, G. (2000): Bevolkingsvraagstukken in Nederland anno 2000 (in Dutch). NIDI, The Hague.

Appendix F. An optimal and preferred EU-15 pension reform strategy[17]

In a report of the European Commission (DG Economic and Financial Affairs) of January 2002 an outline of an optimal and preferred pension reform strategy is given. The optimal strategy is defined as a strategy, that encourages economic growth, reduces budgetary strains and guarantees a fair and a politically sustainable income distribution (generational sustainability). The report is summarized below.

F1 A short history

Public pension expenditures as a percentage of GDP has risen in the EU-15 from about 6 percent in 1960 to over 12 percent in 2000 and, ceteris paribus, could reach levels close to 20 percent of GDP in the coming decades.

The last 40 years has seen little change in the EU-15 in the labour force participation rate. By contrast, the US experienced a 12 to 13 percentage points increase in participation rates. Structural unemployment in the EU-15 increased from 2 percent of the labour force in the 1960's to close to 10 percent by 2000, whilst structural unemployment in the US has been reasonably stable at 5 to 6 percent of the labour force over the last 40 years. In addition, the effective retirement age fell in the EU-15 by 5¼ years to less than 60 over the period 1960-2000 compared with a fall of 3½ years in the US to an average retirement age of 63 over the same period.

As a result the dependency ratio in the EU-15 in 2000 amounted to 26.8 percent opposed to 21.4 percent in the US. As a further result average annual growth rates in the EU-15 decrease from 2¼ percent to 1¾ percent over the next 50 years, representing a cumulative GDP loss of nearly 20 percent. Cumulative reductions of 10 percent are predicted for the US, equivalent to an annual growth loss of around ¼ percentage points over the next 50 years.

Over the past 40 years the number of people aged 65 and over in the EU-15 increased by roughly 28 million and the working age population rose by substantially more, 47 million. In the next 50 years trends change: the number of people over 65 years is growing by an additional 43 million but with the working age population actually declining by 48 million. By comparison, in the US the 65-plus population increases with 47.3 million and the working age population, unlike the EU-15 increases more with 53 million.

In conclusion, the EU-15 will face a more difficult time over the coming decades than the US to address the adverse effects of population aging on the economy.

---

17 McMorrow, K. and W. Roeger [2002]

F2 Scenarios

Assuming that participation rates will stay at their year 2000 levels over the next 50 years, that there are no further reductions in the effective retirement age (now close to 60) and that the net replacement rate also stays at its 2000 level of 74 percent for the next 50 years, the following scenario results are found (*baseline scenario*). The level of per capita GDP in the EU-15 falls by 19 percent over the projection period, with public pension expenditures as a percentage of GDP rising by 7.1 percentage points to 17.6 percent. The equivalent increase in the contributions needed to meet public pension outlays as a percentage of wages is from 16.1 percent in 2000 to nearly 27 percent in 2050. A survey of various scenario findings is presented in table F1.

New projections for the EU-15 have been published in November 2001 by the EU Economic Policy Committee (EPC) over the period 2000-2050, taking account of, first, a large increase in labour force participation by 4 percentage points and a 2 percentage points decline of structural unemployment and, secondly, of a decline of the net replacement rate from 74 percent in 2000 to 58 percent in 2050, a substantial reduction in public pension generosity (to be achieved by some form of price indexation). Using the EPC-assumptions in the present model, K. Mc Morrow and W. Roeger find the following scenario evidence (*M&R scenario*). The level of per capita GDP in the EU-15 falls by 9.2 percent over the projection period (19 percent in the baseline case), with public pension expenditures as a percentage of GDP rising by 3.7 percentage points (7.1 points in the baseline case) to 14.2 percent. The equivalent increase in the contributions needed to meet public pension outlays as a percentage of wages is from 16.1 percent in 2000 to 21.7 percent in 2050 (26.9 percent in the baseline case). Not surprisingly, the reduction of the pension generosity contributes most to the gain in terms of public finance and the labour market reforms contribute most to the gain in terms of economic growth.

To restore equilibrium in the public pension system (fraction of pensions to GDP stabilised at its 2000 level of 10.5 percent) in addition an increase in the effective retirement age to 65 is necessary[18]. A comprehensive package of reform measures {*scenario 'M&R plus retirement age to 65'* (*MR^+ -scenario for short*)} thus entails an increase of per capita GDP (relative to the baseline level) of 26.5 percent, thereby more than offsetting the loss of welfare due to aging (-19 percent). The equilibrium contribution rate paid by workers is stabilised at its 2000 level of 16.1 percent of wages. In terms of income distribution, the working population still fares better than the pensioners due the fall in the net replacement ratio from 74 to 58 percent. Despite this reduction in pension generosity, pensioners will nevertheless see a 13.6 percent increase in their (public pension) income relative to the baseline (-19.5 percent), compared with a gain of 28.3 percent for the working age population (baseline -19.6 percent). Compared with the situation, in

18 The strong budgetary gain is predicated on the crucial assumption that any additional years in employment do not yield any additional pension benefits.

which no aging would have occurred (and not any package of policy measures was introduced), the working age population gains with 8.7 percentage points by 2050, whilst the elderly lose (5.9 percentage points).

F3 An optimal strategy of pension reform and other policy measures in the EU-15

Given that aging will reduce average annual growth rates in the EU-15 from 2¼ percent to 1¾ percent over the next 50 years, it is clear that the key objective of any economic policy strategy primarily must be to reduce these negative growth effects.
Secondly, given that the preferred scenario cannot be achieved over one generation due to a large transition burden, the transition path should be divided into two stages, a partial shift (25 percent) to funding and a 100 percent funded system (public plus private schemes) afterwards.

The first stage, the *optimal scenario* combines the 25 percent move to funding with the latter scenario (*MR^+ -scenario*) aimed at stabilising the transition burden (which is equivalent to stabilising the contribution rate at its year 2000 level). This is achieved by labour market measures, reducing pension generosity (reducing the replacement rate) and bringing back the effective retirement age to 65 year. The case for a shift to funding is the cost advantage for the contribution payer.

The economy of the EU-15 makes a large gain from this reform package with the level of per capita GDP rising by 27.7 percent relative to the baseline scenario by 2050, thereby far more than compensating the negative effects of aging on the EU-15 economy. The largest part of this growth gain arises from labour market reforms and the increase in the retirement age and only a small proportion can be associated with the partial shift to funding. Expenditures on public pay-as-you-go based pensions decline from 10½ percent of GDP in 2000 to 8½ percent by 2050. The equivalent decrease in the contributions needed to meet public pay-as-you-go based pension outlays as a percentage of wages goes from 16.1 percent in 2000 to 12.8 percent in 2050. Contributions to a private funded scheme amount to 2.9 percent of wages. Compared with the comprehensive package of reform measures without a shift to funding per capita GDP by 2050 is 1.2 percentage points higher, total contributions as a percentage of wages are 0.5 points lower and the income distribution is slightly more equal.

The second stage to full funding has only moderate effects on growth, about 0.1 percentage point on an annual average basis, whereas the effects of the package of measures (labour market and retirement age changes) aimed at stabilising the public pension system are likely to yield growth rate gains of about 0.5 percentage points over the next 50 years. Once the transition burden of the shift to a funded system has been cleared (after about 30 years), the equilibrium contribution level of the fully funded system gradually diminishes to 20 to 18 percent of wages, compared with an equilibrium level of 30 to 33 percent for the pay-as-you-go based system in the second half of the 21st century. The discerned scenario results are shown in table F1.

Table F1. Effects of different packages of reform measures in the EU-15 on economic growth, budgetary balance and income distribution

	Economic growth	Budgetary impact		Income distribution	
	p.c. GDP (% change)	public pensions contributions (% wages)	public pensions expenditures (% GDP)	working age population consumption	pensioners consumption
	(1)	(2)	(3)	(4)	(5)
baseline scenario					
2000	0	16.1	10.5	0	0
2030	-12.0	22.9	15.0	-11.9	-15.5
2050	-19.0	26.9	17.6	-19.6	-19.5
M&R scenario					
2000	0	16.1	10.5	0	0
2030	-4.6	19.8	12.9	-2.0	-16.6
2050	-9.2	21.7	14.2	-5.1	-21.2
M&R plus retirement age to 65 (M&R$^+$-scenario)	**(diff. from baseline)**			**(diff. from baseline)**	
2000	0	16.1	10.5	0	0
2030	+17.6	15.6	10.2	+16.2	+12.3
2050	+26.5	16.2	10.6	+28.3	+13.6
optimal scenario (i.e. M&R$^+$ plus 25% shift to funding)	**(diff. from baseline)**		**private pensions contributions (% wages)**	**(diff. from baseline)**	
2000	0	16.1	0	0	0
2030	+18.5	13.3	2.8	+17.1	+12.6
2050	+27.7	12.8	2.9	+29.3	+15.0

In conclusion

Summarizing and concluding, a shift to funding contributes to reducing the premium level paid by workers to meet the pension expenditures and, thus, will bring significant gains in terms of budgetary sustainability. Its contribution to increasing growth, however, is modest, about 0.1 percentage point per year over the next half century. To offset welfare loss and, in contrast, to stimulate increases in production, the shift to funding is accompanied by significant labour market reforms, aimed at boosting labour force participation, reducing structural unemployment and increasing the effective retirement age. Above all measures are taken to enhance labour productivity. Whilst budgetary sustainability is of utmost importance, the central objective for policy makers is encouraging economic growth.

A comprehensive package of reform measures, optimal in the sense of maximising growth and achieving budgetary and income distribution gains, more than compensates the negative effects associated with aging over the next 50 years, takes away fears of public expenditure imbalances and can guarantee that both pensioners and the working age population gain in welfare.

References

Economic Policy Committee/EU (2001): Budgetary challenges posed by ageing populations: the impact on public spending on pensions, health and long-term care for the elderly and possible indicators of the long-term sustainability of public finances, Brussels.

McMorrow, K., Roeger, W. (1999): The economic consequences of ageing populations. Economic Papers no. 138, DG for economic and financial affairs/European Commission, Brussels.

McMorrow, K., Roeger, W. (2002): EU pension reform – an overview of the debate and an empirical assessment of the main policy reform options. Economic Papers no. 162, DG for economic and financial affairs/European Commission, Brussels.

Appendix G . Demography in the EU-15 countries

The demography of all EU-15 member states is shown in Table G1 below.

Table G1. Total population and age distribution in more developed countries, EU-15, US, Canada and Japan in the years 2000, 2020 and 2050: age groups 0-19 year, 20-59 year, 60-64 year and over 65 years of age

	Total population	0-19 y	20-59 y	60-64 y	65^{+} y
	(millions)	(	← percentages →		)
EU-15					
2001	377.8	22.8	55.5	5.4	16.3
2020	384.5	19.5	52.8	6.6	21.1
2050	350.3	18.4	45.5	6.4	29.7
Belgium					
2000	10.2	23.5	54.5	5.2	16.8
2020	10.3	20.5	51.5	7.0	21.0
2050	9.3	19.0	46.3	6.3	28.4
France					
2000	59.3	25.4	54.1	4.5	16.0
2020	61.8	22.0	51.1	6.3	20.6
2050	59.0	19.8	46.8	6.2	27.3
Germany					
2000	82.8	21.4	55.6	6.8	16.3
2020	85.5	18.5	53.1	7.0	21.4
2050	79.7	18.6	46.1	6.8	28.5
Italy					
2000	57.6	19.4	56.6	5.9	18.1
2020	55.5	16.0	53.6	6.8	23.6
2050	45.0	15.6	41.9	6.4	36.1
Netherlands					
2000	15.9	24.2	57.5	4.7	13.6
2020	17.1	20.9	52.7	6.7	19.7
2050	16.7	19.7	47.8	6.1	26.4

Table G1. (continued)

	Total population	0-19 y	20-59 y	60-64 y	65^+ y
	(millions)	(	← percentages →		)
Spain					
2000	40.0	21.2	57.1	4.8	16.9
2020	39.2	17.3	54.7	6.8	21.2
2050	32.6	15.9	41.1	6.1	36.9
Sweden					
2000	8.9	24.1	53.7	4.9	17.3
2020	8.9	19.8	51.3	6.2	22.7
2050	8.4	18.9	47.0	6.8	27.3
UK					
2000	59.5	25.2	54.2	4.9	15.7
2020	61.4	21.4	52.7	6.3	19.6
2050	58.2	19.4	47.2	6.6	26.8
Austria					
2000	8.1	1.8	4.6	0.4	1.3
2020	8.3	1.5	4.5	0.6	1.7
2050	7.7	1.4	3.5	0.5	2.3
Denmark					
2000	5.3	1.3	3.0	0.3	0.8
2020	5.6	1.2	2.9	0.4	1.1
2050	5.6	1.2	2.7	0.3	1.4
Finland					
2000	5.2	1.3	2.9	0.3	0.8
2020	5.2	1.1	2.6	0.4	1.2
2050	4.7	0.9	2.2	0.3	1.3
Greece					
2000	10.6	2.3	5.8	0.6	1.8
2020	10.6	2.0	5.6	0.7	2.3
2050	9.2	1.6	4.0	0.6	3.1
Ireland					
2000	3.8	1.2	2.1	0.2	0.4
2020	4.4	1.1	2.3	0.2	0.7
2050	4.5	0.9	2.1	0.3	1.1

Table G1. (continued)

	Total population	0-19 y	20-59 y	60-64 y	65^{+} y
	(millions)	(	← percentages →		)
Luxemburg					
2000	0.4	0.1	0.3	0.0	0.1
2020	0.5	0.1	0.3	0.0	0.1
2050	0.6	0.1	0.3	0.1	0.1
Portugal					
2000	10.1	2.4	5.6	0.5	1.6
2020	10.1	2.1	5.4	0.6	2.0
2050	9.0	1.7	4.1	0.5	2.8

Source: the U.S. Department of the Census; data can be downloaded from http://www.census.gov/ipc/www/idbprint.html. Note that projections until the middle of the 21st century are subject to wide margins of error. Marked differences exist between forecasts of UN, Eurostat and the Census Bureau.